Professional Practice in Governance and Public Organizations

"Professional Practice in Governance and Public Organizations" offers cutting-edge insights and practical guidance for professionals in the areas of economics, politics, public policy and public administration, and those working at international organizations. The series features concise and accessible books on the latest developments in governance, organizational and political strategies, institutional policies, policy instruments, public management, and finance. Leadership and digitalization issues are a core topic throughout the series. All volumes are written by practitioners, experts and leading authorities from think tanks, non-governmental organizations, and public and international organizations. While the books are explicitly intended for professionals in the above-mentioned fields, students of economics, political science, public policy and public administration will also benefit from these practical guides for their future careers.

Dirk Ehnts

Modern Money Theory

A Simple Guide to the Monetary System

Dirk Ehnts
Berlin, Germany

ISSN 2731-9776 ISSN 2731-9784 (electronic)
Professional Practice in Governance and Public Organizations
ISBN 978-3-031-53536-9   ISBN 978-3-031-53537-6 (eBook)
https://doi.org/10.1007/978-3-031-53537-6

© The Editor(s) (if applicable) and The Author(s), under exclusive license to Springer Nature Switzerland AG 2024

This work is subject to copyright. All rights are solely and exclusively licensed by the Publisher, whether the whole or part of the material is concerned, specifically the rights of reprinting, reuse of illustrations, recitation, broadcasting, reproduction on microfilms or in any other physical way, and transmission or information storage and retrieval, electronic adaptation, computer software, or by similar or dissimilar methodology now known or hereafter developed.
The use of general descriptive names, registered names, trademarks, service marks, etc. in this publication does not imply, even in the absence of a specific statement, that such names are exempt from the relevant protective laws and regulations and therefore free for general use.
The publisher, the authors, and the editors are safe to assume that the advice and information in this book are believed to be true and accurate at the date of publication. Neither the publisher nor the authors or the editors give a warranty, expressed or implied, with respect to the material contained herein or for any errors or omissions that may have been made. The publisher remains neutral with regard to jurisdictional claims in published maps and institutional affiliations.

This Springer imprint is published by the registered company Springer Nature Switzerland AG
The registered company address is: Gewerbestrasse 11, 6330 Cham, Switzerland

Paper in this product is recyclable.

Praise for *Modern Money Theory*

"I very much enjoyed working with Dirk on a variety of segments of his latest book. It's one of the very few that is fundamentally grounded in an understanding of monetary operations as practiced by all central banks, which gives the reader a sound basis for the analysis of today's monetary economies."
—Warren Mosler, *Inventor of Modern Money Theory*

"Ehnts' no-nonsense introduction to MMT gets into the most up-to-date consequences of the COVID-19 crisis and government responses."
—Maren Poitras, *Director "Finding the Money"*

"This compact introduction to all aspects of modern monetary theory is an exemplary work of popular science. The author, Dirk Ehnts, is a brilliant communicator, Europe's answer to Stephanie Kelton, and the book is an accessible and comprehensive guide to the first major challenge to mainstream macroeconomics in 70 years."
—Steven Hail, *adjunct associate professor at Torrens University Australia*

"Offering a sober analysis of the monetary system, this book should be on the desk of every public and government employee."
—Stephanie Kelton, *professor of economics and public policy at Stony Brook University*

Contents

1 **Introduction**   1
2 **The Biden Administration and the Copernican Turn**   3
    2.1 Can the Federal Government Run Out of Money?   5
    2.2 Political Constraints of Government Spending   13
    2.3 Government Spending, the Public Deficit, and Inflation   17
    2.4 Monetary Policy, Inflation, and Financial Instability   21
3 **The Paper Currency of Virginia (1760s) and Its Lessons**   29
    3.1 Provisioning the State and Money Printing   33
    3.2 Tax Revenues Are not "Financing" the Government   40
    3.3 Drafting a Federal Budget   43
4 **Modern Money Theory as Part of Economics**   49
    4.1 The Failing Monetary Policy of Inflation Targeting   52
    4.2 Government Spending   55
    4.3 Government Bonds   58
    4.4 International Trade   65
    4.5 Sectoral Balances, Exchange Rates, and Unit Labor Costs   69
5 **What is Economic Policy?**   73
    5.1 Theory and Practice   74
    5.2 The Circular Flow of Income   75
    5.3 The Modern Business Cycle   83
    5.4 Banking and Banking Regulation   88

6	**Economic Policies Based on MMT**	97
	6.1 How Do We Ensure Full Employment?	98
	6.2 How Do We Ensure Price Stability?	102
	6.3 The Job Guarantee	108
	6.4 Industrial Policy	110
	6.5 A Green New Deal	112
	6.6 Inequality and Climate Justice	118
	6.7 An Economic Bill of Rights for the Twenty-First Century	120
7	**Outlook**	123
Literature		127

1

Introduction

Modern Money Theory (or Modern Monetary Theory; MMT) has been around for more than a quarter of a century. Thinking about questions of money and economics in general is not something we usually do, and for the most part it requires a special occasion. For Warren Mosler, the founder of Modern Money Theory, the crucial occasion was the economic crisis in Italy in the early 1990s.[1] Italian government bonds, issued in Italian lira, were under severe downward pressure. Investors feared that the government would not be able to repay the government bonds at maturity and therefore tried to sell them.[2] This caused their price to fall.

In fact, Italian government debt was more than one hundred percent of Italy's economic output (also called GDP, gross domestic product). But did that imply the Italian government would run out of money? Mosler observed that the Italian government was always able to service their government bonds at maturity and unapologetically issued new ones. He came to the conclusion that it apparently had no payment problem as long as its own central bank supported it—which it did, of course. He wrote down these ideas and other insights, published a small book, and sought contact with professional economists.[3] This was the beginning of what is now called Modern Money Theory—MMT.[4]

---

[1] See Mosler (2017, 139).
[2] It is a coincidence that both currencies were called *lira*.
[3] See https://econpapers.repec.org/paper/wpawuwpma/9502007.htm.
[4] This happened in the mid-1990s. Originally, MMT was short for Modern Money Theory, following Keynes (1930) who in his first pages discussed that in modern states money would be Chartalist (created by the state). Sometimes, Modern Monetary Theory is used instead.

© The Author(s), under exclusive license to Springer Nature Switzerland AG 2024
D. Ehnts, *Modern Money Theory*, Professional Practice in Governance and Public Organizations, https://doi.org/10.1007/978-3-031-53537-6_1

The first to engage with Warren Mosler's ideas were Stephanie Kelton, Pavlina Tcherneva, Randall Wray, Bill Mitchell, Mat Forstater, Martin Watts, and Scott Fullwiler. They were later joined by Yeva Nersisyan, Fadhel Kaboub, Rohan Grey, and Christine Desan.[5] These scholars wrote academic articles, books, and internet blogs and published videos to promote their new theory of money. Today, MMT is popular in the US, with proposals such as the Green New Deal and the Job Guarantee being debated in public. A MMT conference is held every year, in 2018 at the New School for Social Research in New York and in 2019 at Stony Brook University. In February 2019, I organized the 1st International European MMT Conference in Berlin on behalf of the non-profit Samuel-Pufendorf Society for Political Economy, and the second was held on September 13–15, 2021.[6] This was followed by a 3rd conference on September 9–10, 2023. MMT is now also being discussed in Germany and Europe.[7]

In 2010, I met Randall Wray at a conference in Berlin, who drew my attention to the MMT blogs New Economic Perspectives and Billy blog.[8] I commented on the chapters he presented online and offered to translate the book (Wray 2014) into German. However, the publisher did not like the idea, so I decided to write my own book on money creation in the Eurozone. This resulted in "Geld und Kredit: Eine €-päische Perspektive" (Money and Credit: A €-uropean Perspective), which was published in 2014. In 2016, an English translation was published under the title "Modern Monetary Theory and European Macroeconomics". What has been missing on the market so far is a compact introduction to the theory, basic assumptions, and economic policy conclusions of MMT. This book aims to fill this gap. It is aimed at academics, students, practitioners in financial markets, and all other readers interested in the topic. Special thanks go to Phil Armstrong for commenting on the manuscript. All remaining errors are mine.

---

[5] See Mosler (1995, 1998, 2017), Kelton (2020), Tcherneva (2020), Wray et al. (2019), Mitchell and Muysken (2008), Mitchell (2017), Mitchell and Fazi (2017), Forstater and Murray (2013), Fullwiler (2017), Nersisyan and Wray (2021), Kaboub (2007), Grey (2020), and Desan (2014).

[6] Videos are available at https://www.pufendorf-gesellschaft.org/mmt21.

[7] See https://www.focus.de/finanzen/boerse/ezb-soll-den-staat-finanzieren-oekonom-kaempft-fuer-ein-ende-des-schulden-mantras_id_12395457.html and https://www.zeit.de/2019/15/stephanie-kelton-modern-monetary-theory-staatsschulden-usa. Ehnts (2017, 2022) and Höfgen (2020) have published introductions to MMT in German, and there is also a textbook on macroeconomics (Ehnts 2023). I sought an explanation for money after publishing my Ph.D. dissertation on economic geography (Ehnts 2008).

[8] See http://neweconomicperspectives.org and http://bilbo.economicoutlook.net/blog/.

2

The Biden Administration and the Copernican Turn

In 2021, the economy was supposed to gain steam after a pandemic with lockdowns, followed by a large-scale vaccination campaign. Hampered by the lockdowns and other measures, as well as the fact that shopping in stores was simply not allowed for weeks on end, all companies combined had produced less in 2020 than they had in 2019. Demand for workers was lower, and companies laid off workers. This applied to just about every country on our planet. In April 2020, the official unemployment rate was 14.8%.[1] Now, however, there was a problem. Those who were involuntarily unemployed received very little money and only for a short time. But if the unemployed workers had less income, how could they maintain their level of consumption? They couldn't, and so the companies realized that they would no longer be able to sell all of their output.

Price cuts and wage reductions were ruled out as remedies by theoretical considerations. Lower prices might lead to higher sales, but profits would collapse and companies would have trouble paying back the debts (loans, bonds, etc.) they used to finance their production. While lower wages theoretically increase profits for a single firm, they also reduce demand for goods and services as workers earn less. The economy would end up in a vicious circle. It was clear that private companies needed help if they were to bring their production back up to pre-crisis levels. There was too little spending in the economy, and companies had reduced output. If left unchecked, the vicious

---

[1] https://fred.stlouisfed.org/series/UNRATE.

circle would have led to more and more US workers becoming unemployed, and hence businesses would have continued to cut production because there just wasn't enough demand. The idea of an equilibrium in the market, with sellers and buyers satisfied with supply and demand, had to be abandoned. In a crisis, it becomes obvious to all that the market does not regulate itself, but collapses in a downward spiral. When it stabilizes, it will be at a lower level of output with mass unemployment and no tendency to move back to full employment. The economy is not a self-equilibrating system that can or should be left on autopilot. The economy needs supervision and management.

Economic policy for stabilization

The federal government has been using macroeconomic policy since 1933, when it dealt with the Great Depression. Back then, the Great Crash of 1929 caused mass unemployment as the stock market crashed in parallel with the real estate market. So, the Biden administration knew that government action was needed to help the economy recover. When businesses are pessimistic, they want to save more and invest less. They are afraid they will not be able to pay back loans to banks and bonds to investors. This would plunge many companies into insolvency—not a pretty outlook. So, the companies tried to reduce their expenditures. They cut back on investments in capacity and productivity, which probably had little chance of making money anyway due to the weak demand for their products. From the perspective of a single company, that is all rational.

This, however, led to a problem. When companies cut spending, they cut income elsewhere. After all, one company's spending might be another's income. (Think about parts delivered by one company that are used by another to produce a consumption good.) Also, companies spend money on workers. If workers lose income and spend less, then a reduction in saving elsewhere in the economy results. Firms and households save out of income, and every reduction in income must by definition lead to a loss in saving (defined as unspent income). The relative improvement of one firm, which now has higher savings (because it saved more), leads to a loss of income and saving(s) for another economic unit (firm or household). Since workers spend significantly less with reduced income and reduced saving, the macroeconomic results would be disastrous. So, it was no surprise that in April 2020 the official unemployment rate reached 14.7%. More than 23 million Americans were unemployed. Including underemployment (which includes workers working part-time but want full-time jobs), the rate was even higher: 22.9%![2] In December 2019, 12.8 million manufacturing jobs existed. By April 2020, that number was down to 11.4 million—almost 1.5 million manufacturing workers were thrown out of their jobs. Put differently, the US economy lost all manufacturing jobs added since 2010 in just five months!

The economists in the Biden administration understood this. The US federal government would have to step in and stabilize the economy by increasing government spending. Buying more goods and services, the US government created additional demand. In doing so, it stabilized existing jobs and created new ones. Companies responded by expanding production and hiring workers again. This had an effect on the wider economy, because now more workers had jobs again and consumed more, which in turn caused companies to hire more workers. The vicious circle was broken, the economy recovered. By December 2021, the unemployment rate was back at 3.9%. Less than 6 million Americans were unemployed. In December 2022, the US economy had more manufacturing jobs than before the pandemic. The US government avoided a repeat of the Great Depression. At its height in 1933, four year after the Great Crash, almost a quarter of the workforce was out of work. The New Deal by FDR created the modern welfare state that still forms the backbone of the US economy.

2.1 Can the Federal Government Run Out of Money?

The big question is a theoretical one: can the Biden administration simply increase government spending to the desired amount? The 2021 *American Rescue Plan* included spending worth $1.9 trillion, the 2021 *Build Back Better Act* $2.2 trillion, the 2022 *CHIPS and Science Act* was worth $280 billion, and the 2022 *Inflation Reduction Act* was worth $738 billion. By now, we know what the correct answer is. The federal government can simply increase government spending by the desired amount. Since its creation in 1776, the US government has never run out of US dollars. Nevertheless, in the early phase of the pandemic there was a lot of doubt about the capabilities of the federal government to spend money. Since tax revenues had plummeted in the aftermath of the economic crisis triggered by the pandemic, Washington was running a fiscal deficit of nearly 20% of GDP in the second quarter of

---

[2] https://fred.stlouisfed.org/series/U6RATE.

2020![3] The question therefore arose as to whether the US government would be able to "finance" its deficits without any problems.

A 2019 survey by the Initiative on Global Markets at the Booth School of Business at the University of Chicago confronted participating economists with the statement: "Countries that borrow in their own currency should not worry about government deficits because they can always create money to finance their debt".[4] Of the more than forty economists who responded not a single one expressed agreement, 36% disagreed with the statement, and 52% strongly disagreed with the statement. A few had no opinion, and 10% did not respond.

If those economists had been right, the Biden administration's position would have been highly problematic. It might not have been able to finance its additional spending. This would have rendered a government response to the economic crisis impossible because it would probably have resulted in the US government defaulting on its "public debt". Investors would have dumped US government bonds, interest rates would have risen, and bankruptcy would have been inevitable. Politicians, dependent on the financial markets and "China" (for buying bonds), would have had to capitulate. However, things turned out quite differently. (We'll get to the debt ceiling later.) The USA was not exceptional. In the Eurozone, the Greek government watched their public debt to GDP ratio approach Japanese levels. In early 2020, it stood at more than 210% of GDP, much higher than the 135% of GDP that US public debt to GDP was at the time. Greece did not run out of money (euros) as the European Commission deactivated the overly strict fiscal deficit targets of 3% of GDP and the European Central Bank effectively made the Eurozone's government bonds risk-free with a huge asset purchase program.[5]

New economic policy

As we have seen, the Biden administration passed several spending packages to combat the crisis and repair infrastructure, each worth trillions (thousands of billions) of dollars. At times, the federal government's account balance at the Federal Reserve Bank was nearly 2 trillion dollars.[6] This was not technically necessary, but it shows what is possible. The price of US government bonds remained unchanged, with the Federal Reserve, like the ECB,

---

[3] https://covid19policy.adb.org/sector-financial-balances/economies.
[4] https://www.igmchicago.org/surveys/modern-monetary-theory/.
[5] See Ehnts and Paetz (2021) for the details of the Eurozone's response to the pandemic and Ehnts (2017) for a description of the Eurozone from a MMT perspective.
[6] https://fred.stlouisfed.org/series/FGCDCAQ027S.

launching a purchase program.[7] The financial markets remained completely calm, and there was never any discussion of government insolvency.[8] By mid-2023, the result of *Bidenomics* was clear. The US economy was back on the growth path—not the growth path of the lackluster 2010s, but that of the 2000s![9]

Figure 2.1 shows personal consumption expenditures in billions of dollars. In the 2000s, personal consumption expenditures increased at a trend shown by the dotted line. When the Global Financial Crisis hit, personal consumption expenditures collapsed. During the recovery these expenditures started to grow again, but there was a gap between the old trend and the new trend. This gap measures roughly 500 billion dollars (!) of foregone consumption a year. Back in the early 2010s, there was a debate among economists. The economic adviser to President Obama, Larry Summers, claimed that the economy would be held back by supply side constraints. He dug out the old concept of *secular stagnation*, introduced by Alvin Hansen in the 1930s during the Great Depression.[10] Looking at Fig. 2.1, Summers was saying that there was nothing that could be done to close that 500 billion dollars gap. The US economy would permanently produce less than before.

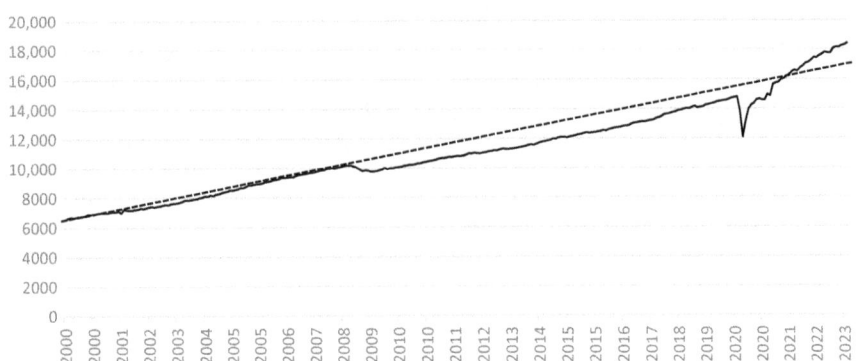

Fig. 2.1 Personal consumption expenditures in billions of dollars. *Source* https://fred.stlouisfed.org/series/PCE

---

[7] See Clarida et al. (2021, 4).

[8] Only in fall 2021 there was a debate on debt sustainability in the context of the debt ceiling. One idea was to mint a trillion-dollar coin to avoid the debt ceiling: See https://www.washingtonpost.com/business/2021/10/05/trillion-dollar-coin-faq/.

[9] This is not an endorsement of *Bidenomics*, which could and should have gone much beyond a change in macroeconomic management. However, it was a good choice not to listen to Larry Summers and others who called for higher unemployment to reduce inflation. That would have been the wrong strategy.

[10] https://larrysummers.com/imf-fourteenth-annual-research-conference-in-honor-of-stanley-fischer/.

The other camp disagreed with this view. If only the government would spend more money, more goods and services would be produced by workers that were at the time unemployed or underemployed. Hence the gap was caused by a policy mistake which, over ten years, led to a loss of production and consumption in the US economy—a whopping 5-trillion-dollar mistake that could have been avoided with better policy advice. The US economy in the 2010s could have produced all the valuable goods and services that were consumed plus an extra 500 billion US dollars' worth of goods and service, going perhaps into upgrading and expanding crumbling infrastructure. About 500 billion dollars' worth of spending is quite a lot!

So, the Biden administration was right to spend a lot of dollars on upgrading infrastructure and other things that needed fixing. There seemed to be no limit to the trillions of dollars that the federal government could spend. Before that happened, in 2020, it had driven its debt level from 108% of gross domestic product (GDP) to 136% of GDP within a single quarter! How could it be that a 28% point increase in the national debt to GDP level within three months did not have a massive negative impact on the economy? Why were the effects positive? (At the time, some economists pointed out that inflation resulted, but at the end of 2023 we know that this was not connected—the inflation was transitory.)

Confronted with reality, the old theory of public finance collapsed. Apparently, the US federal government can't run out of money. The idea that the federal government's budget would be anything like the budget of a household had to be abandoned. A Copernican turn occurred, because the empirical facts, which were known for a long time, were now seen in a different light. The lens that made that possible is called Modern Money Theory (MMT). A theory is supposed to explain reality, and MMT does it better than the older theories dealing with macroeconomic issues, like interest rates, inflation, unemployment and government spending. MMT is not a policy proposal or something that can be "applied" or "imposed". While the core of MMT consists of an examination of monetary operations, a proper understanding of the monetary mechanics obviously leads to ideas on how to improve the system.

Before Modern Money Theory is explained in the remaining chapters, a few quotes from the chairman of the US House of Representatives Budget Committee, Democrat John Yarmuth of Kentucky, will serve as a sneak preview. In June 2021, he was asked about deficits and the national debt in an interview with C-SPAN, the House's television network.[11] The transcript traces the interview[12]:

Greta Brawner: *So, Chair Yarmuth, how can we spend $6 trillion, and all the other money President Biden wants to spend? How can we afford it?*

John Yarmuth: *We can afford it, because we determine how much money is in the system—at the federal level. The federal government is not like any other user of currency, not like any household, any business, any state or local government. We issue our own currency, and we can spend enough to meet the needs of the American people—the only constraint being that we do have to worry about inflation from that spending.*

Now, so many people say that we have so much debt, and our grandchildren—it is going to be on their backs, and so forth. That is not the way it works. And I think the American people need an education about how the monetary system does work. I remember going back, Greta, to when Paul Ryan was chair of the Budget Committee, and even before that—and all of these forecasts of gloom and doom about "Oh, we are going to accumulate so much debt, and interest rates are going to crowd out all other spending." Well, we basically doubled the national debt from the recession in 2009 until last year, before the pandemic. And none of the things that people warned would happen, happened. We didn't have inflation. We had record low interest rates, rather than higher interest rates. And the dollar was trading with normal levels, vis-a-vis other currencies.

So, I think a lot of economists have begun to say "wait a minute"—"Maybe we have been thinking about debt in entirely the wrong way. Even Fed Chair Jay Powell has basically said "We have the fiscal space to do what we need to do right now to make the investments we need to make—to build the kind of economy for the future we all hope we will have."

Greta Brawner: *Well, why are people wrong about this? How should we be thinking about debt and deficits?*

John Yarmuth: *Well, I don't get any royalties from this, but I would flog a work called "The Deficit Myth," by Stephanie Kelton—an economist and professor.*[13] *And it's become quite a bestseller, actually. What she says is that, "If you look at the total national debt, $28 trillion right now," what we think of as the national*

---

[11] https://www.c-span.org/video/?512625-5/washington-journal-rep-john-yarmuth-D-ky-discusses-president-bidens-fy-2022-budget-request&event=512625&playEvent.
[12] https://medium.com/@KellyGerling/rep-john-yarmuth-D-ky-03-talks-about-mmt-to-answer-what-do-the-american-people-need-us-to-do-da9a4f84ec98.
[13] See Kelton (2020).

debt, she said, "Don't think of it as debt. Think of it as all the money the federal government has invested in the country over our history—minus taxes." And that's really what it is. I mean, those $28 trillion didn't exist—before the federal government issued them. And so, the federal government has the ability to create money, create financing, and that's what we've been doing and will continue to do.

The thing I am so impressed about from the Biden Administration is that they're reversing decades and decades of our asking questions in the wrong order. Historically, what we've always done is said, "What can we afford to do?" And that's not the right question. The right question is, "What do the American People need us to do?" And that question becomes the first question. Once you've answered that, then you say, "How do you resource that need?".

That's not just money—that's also capacity.

So, for instance, there is a $225 billion investment in childcare in the American Families Plan. But you can't just say we're going to give $225 billion to people to pay for their childcare, because there's not enough capacity. So, what you'd do [hypothetically] is, you'd make a false promise to the people, and then you would drive the price of existing childcare even higher. So, what you have to do, is spend part of that money on building capacity so that there is enough childcare to actually service the people who need it.

The first important point is the distinction between users of money and issuers (creators) of money. In the first paragraph, Yarmuth explains that the US federal government can determine how much money it wants to create with its spending. Inflation can be a problem, but scarcity of money apparently cannot. In the second paragraph, after a reference to MMT economist Stephanie Kelton's bestselling book (which is a great longer read that I can recommend with my whole heart), Yarmuth explains that there is no "national debt" in the sense that the government has to "pay back" its "debtors". The 28 trillion dollars usually referred to as "public debt" would simply be the money spent by the US government that has not been recovered through taxes yet. The US government, Yarmuth continued, can and does create money. It does not need to worry about running out of money for technical reasons.

The Copernican Turn

MMT thus enables us to perform the Copernican turn mentioned above. Government spending, tax revenues, government bond revenues, interest rates, and inflation—we already knew about all this. Now we see it from a new perspective. The central insight is that the state has a monopoly on money. Just as a movie theater cannot run out of tickets, a federal government cannot run out of its own money. Of course, this does not mean that it should spend an infinite amount of it! No cinema would sell an infinite amount of cinema tickets because these need to be redeemed. The insight is that there is no scarcity of money for the government. The question of how government spending is paid for can be answered very simply: with public money, the US dollar, which is newly created through spending. The details will be explained in later chapters.

The new perspective also debunks as a myth the notion that "the taxpayer" finances government spending.[14] Since the government is always creating new money as it spends, tax payments do not serve to finance it. In the same way, government bonds do not finance the federal government. In reality, the government is "self-financing". We could say that it finances itself with money creation by its central bank, the Federal Reserve Bank. Before the federal government can spend, it is forced by political rules to have a positive balance in its account at the Fed. That account is a balance for internal purposes as the federal government cannot own "money", which is its own I.O.U. (I owe you). Such rules require a particular sequence of financial transactions but have no operational significance.[15]

For each dollar, the federal government owes us a reduction of tax liabilities of the amount printed on the bank note or the amount transferred electronically. US dollar bills read: "Legal Tender for All Debts, Public and Private". Our tax liabilities are the public debts mentioned here. So, modern money for us is nothing but a tax credit, allowing us to get rid of tax liabilities. In the hands of the federal government, which cannot and does not make tax payments or other payments to itself, this special I.O.U. loses its legal power. Having returned to the issuer, the I.O.U. once again becomes a piece of paper (or, today, a rather meaningless number in an account at the Fed). This is how most paper currencies started, having been printed by the Bureau of Engraving and Printing and being owned by the central bank during its "youth".[16] Only when cash is spent into the economy does it count as "money". However, when the government spends today, it does not pay cash. It pays using the electronic payment system—with digital dollars!

The government's account at the Federal Reserve is credited when bond revenues and tax revenues come in and debited when the Treasury spends.

---

[14] "The taxpayer" is often thought to be white and male, so it is a somewhat racist framing. See https://www.motherjones.com/politics/2021/04/taxpayer-dollars-the-origins-of-austeritys-racist-catchphrase/.

[15] Explained below (see Wray 2012).

[16] The NY Times ran a nice article on money printing in early 2023, nicely visualizing the process: https://www.nytimes.com/interactive/2023/02/26/us/printing-money-treasury.html.

The Fed is only allowed to act as fiscal agent of the state when the Treasury General Account is in the black. Tax and government bond revenues help to fulfill this political requirement. Since the banks have to pay with central bank deposits (hereafter called *reserves*, sometimes also called *settlement balances*), the creation of reserves has to happen first. Since only the Fed can create reserves, the state has to spend first—only later can the dollars thus created be used for tax and bond payments. (This does not mean that tax payments and taxes in general do not matter. It just means that their purpose is not financing the government.)

The imposition of tax liabilities causes goods and services to be offered for sale, presumably to the government, which can buy them with its otherwise worthless currency. This leads to what economists call a demand for money and ensures the "acceptance" of a currency.[17] It also helps to preserve democracy by preventing extreme inequality of income and wealth. Without tax liabilities imposed on us by the state we might not accept payments in our currency at all. Why should we offer labor or goods and services for our domestic currency? There are already enough currencies, it seems. Why don't we all just use the British pound, like in the years before the Declaration of Independence in 1776, or the Canadian dollar? Or the Euro? It is the tax liabilities in national currency that the state forces upon us which creates a demand for US dollars. Sure, most of us will accept dollars because others do. Someone, however, must have had a reason for doing so in the first place and that reason is usually tax liabilities in national currency. This, at least, is what the monetary history of the British colonies in America tells us, as we will see later.

Government bonds are also not used for "financing". The buyers of the government bonds virtually exchange reserves (on which the Fed pays interest) for (more profitable but less liquid) interest-bearing bonds. This reduces the quantity of reserves and, possibly, increases the interest rate on the interbank market. More reserves—resulting from more government spending—should drive the interest rate down. Government bond issuance thus serves to stabilize the interest rate on the interbank market. Since banks can only buy government bonds with government money (reserves), the government must first put reserves into circulation before these return via government bond revenues and tax revenues. This is what the French root of the word "revenue" (to come back) implies: money *returns* to the issuer.

So, the federal government cannot run out of dollars for technical reasons. The chairman of the Fed, Alan Greenspan, affirmed this in front of Congress

---

[17] Acceptance of the currency is what matters. That acceptance can be lost. More on this later.

and under oath in 2005, when he was questioned about the feasibility of private pension plans to support public pensions, stating that "there is nothing to prevent the federal government from creating as much money as it wants and paying it to somebody".[18] This does not mean that the federal government cannot tie its hands on its back by legislating political rules that make it impossible to spend more money under certain conditions. The debt ceiling is one such rule (out of many). The CUTGO (formerly PAYGO) rule in Congress is another.[19] Let's have a look.

2.2 Political Constraints of Government Spending

The US government, while not constrained technically, is constrained in its spending politically. First and foremost, there is the budgeting process. The federal government cannot spend US dollars on anything it wants. If it wants to spend, the spending has to be included in the federal budget, which is passed by the Congress. Only then can the Treasury instruct the Fed to make payments on its behalf. This, then, is the main political constraint with respect to government spending. However, there is more. The debt ceiling and the CUTGO rule make life harder for the federal government.

The debt ceiling

The debt ceiling, officially the debt limit, "is the total amount of money that the United States government is authorized to borrow to meet its existing legal obligations, including Social Security and Medicare benefits, military salaries, interest on the national debt, tax refunds, and other payments", according to the Treasury.[20] It restricts the public debt to a nominal number of US dollars. Since the federal government needs to pre-finance its spending (selling government bonds to create a positive balance in its account at the Fed), hitting the debt ceiling would stop the government from spending more than tax revenues.[21] This is because the federal government would not be allowed to sell any more bonds, given that the debt ceiling is reached. The

---

[18] https://www.youtube.com/watch?v=DNCZHAQnfGU.
[19] https://crsreports.congress.gov/product/pdf/R/R41510.
[20] https://home.treasury.gov/policy-issues/financial-markets-financial-institutions-and-fiscal-service/debt-limit.
[21] In the Eurozone, national governments spend first and then bring their account's balance back to zero or positive.

government's account at the Fed thus cannot move up into positive territory by selling more bonds. Instead, the government has to wait for tax revenues to replenish the account. This arrangement has been created for purely political reasons. The Fed is only allowed to credit accounts with reserves when the government's account is positive.

We often imagine that the federal government can have "money", but that is not possible. Since US dollars are ultimately a tax credit that can be used by citizens to discharge their liabilities against the state, they are worthless when returned to the government. Therefore, money in the hands of the state has no legal force. The Fed does not "owe" the government money. It owes money creation on behalf of the Treasury because that is what the law says. Tax revenues are also recorded on the government's account at the Fed, which is called the Treasury General Account. When the debt ceiling is reached, the government is forced to limit its spending to its tax revenues, which is an artificial and political limitation. The real constraint is what the private sector offers for sale. The federal government can buy that and not more—at least not domestically.

To increase the debt ceiling, both houses of Congress have to agree to it. A simple majority suffices. Often, the federal government does not have a majority in both the House of Representatives and the Senate. This gives a lot of power to the opposition party, which can demand political reforms as a price for agreeing to increase the debt ceiling. The opposition could also use its power to push the US into default, but that has never happened. So, the debt ceiling is a strange construction. It was established by the Public Debt Acts of 1939 and 1941. It might be unconstitutional as it potentially stops the government from performing its duties. It is a strange idea to have a democracy where the federal government cannot spend what it budgeted to spend. Why vote for a federal government if it cannot spend the dollars needed?

Given that the Fed is the fiscal agent of the state, it is not clear whether the US politicians would be allowed to push the USA into default. One possibility for the Fed to prevent government default would be to buy defaulted Treasury bonds at full price, as Nathan Tankus argued in a piece for Politico and on his blog.[22] Here is a dialogue between then-Chairman Ben Bernanke and Jerome Powell, who succeeded him (options 8 and 9 refer to the Fed buying and swapping defaulted Treasury bonds):

---

[22] See https://www.politico.com/news/magazine/2023/04/19/powell-debt-ceiling-fed-00092522 and https://www.crisesnotes.com/more-foia-findings-the-new-nixon-administrations-debt-ceiling-dilemma-and-the-federal-reserves-solutions/?ref=notes-on-the-crises-newsletter.

MR. POWELL: *As long as I'm talking, I find 8 and 9 to be loathsome. I hope that gets into the minutes. [Laughter] But I don't want to say today what I would and wouldn't do, if we have to actually deal with a catastrophe on this.*

CHAIRMAN BERNANKE: *So, you are willing to accept "loathsome" under some certain circumstances. [Laughter]*

MR. POWELL: *Yes, under certain circumstances.*

If the Fed would treat defaulted Treasury bonds as non-defaulted Treasury bonds, investors would be assured that they can always get their US dollars. Since they can sell Treasury bonds to the Fed any time in return for reserves, they would still be happy to hold Treasury bonds. Since the Fed cannot run out of money, it could promise to buy up all Treasury bonds and all other debt instruments of the US government if it has to. This would de facto avoid default on US Treasury bonds and allow the federal government to sell "defaulted" bonds to the banks, so it could spend money again.

The trillion-dollar platinum coin

The trillion-dollar platinum coin would be another solution. Atlanta lawyer Carlos Mucha came up with the idea, commenting on a blog.[23] He found that a law existed that would allow the Treasury to mint platinum coins of any denomination. The Treasury would deposit that coin at the Federal Reserve, which would then credit its account. Problem solved! The government could continue to spend money without having to raise the debt limit. Of course, this solution would completely invalidate the debt ceiling. It is a second-best solution in case the political situation does not allow a better solution. However, we can learn from this that monetary rules matter. Changing monetary rules is clearly within the limits of policymaking. Why not have a debate about which monetary rules serve Americans best? Today's rules seem to be skewed toward decreasing government spending. Another modern rule is the CUTGO rule, which has replaced the PAYGO rule.

The CUTGO rule

---

[23] https://nymag.com/intelligencer/2023/05/the-man-who-invented-the-trillion-dollar-coin.html.

The House cut-as-you-go (CUTGO) rule is generally intended to discourage or prevent Congress from taking certain legislative action that would increase the fiscal deficit, as the Congressional Research Service writes.[24] It prohibits the consideration of legislation that is estimated to increase mandatory spending over either a six-year period or an 11-year period. The rule requires legislation that includes provisions estimated to increase mandatory spending to include offsetting reductions in other mandatory spending. (It does not apply to discretionary spending or revenues.) According to Congress, examples of programs funded through mandatory spending include Medicare, unemployment compensation, and the federal employee retirement system. This means that any increase in government spending in these areas will have to be offset by a cut in government spending elsewhere.

Just as with the debt ceiling, it is not clear what this political rule is supposed to accomplish. The whole point of a democracy is that the federal government can use its budget to create the public goods and services it has promised to provide. There is no a-priori reason to force a government to reduce the provisions of public goods and services when it expands them elsewhere. No other Western government has such a rule.[25]

One important political question concerns the size of the government. Many commentators feel that the government tends to increase in size over time and they believe that this is a bad thing. Therefore, they want rules that limit the size of the government. This, however, creates a conflict with democratic governance. The government exists to provide its citizens with public goods and services. Its role in our society is absolutely fundamental. Without US dollars, the state's currency issued by its central bank, and property rights, backed up by law enforcement and the justice system, there would be no "market". Why bother going to a market if no money can be had or only money of dubious purchasing power? And why go to a market if somebody can just take your goods and services by force?

The government also plays a large role in helping workers to educate themselves and to gain skills and knowledge. It ensures that citizens are free from fear by providing basic public goods and services: roads and traffic lights, kindergarten and schools, trains and subways, health care, and pensions (at least to some of its citizens). There is nothing wrong with the government providing those public goods and services. Government spending is limited by available resources offered for sale. The government cannot hire more workers than are available and looking for paid work (in the currency of the

---

[24] https://crsreports.congress.gov/product/pdf/R/R41510.

[25] That does not mean that there are no political rules that constrain government spending elsewhere. Europe and the Eurozone have lots of debt brakes and fiscal frameworks that do so.

state). It also understands that every worker hired to work in the public sector will not be available to work in the private sector. There is no free lunch, at least not in economic terms. The US dollars that are created by the Fed, however, cost (next to) nothing.

To succeed economically, the federal government should be bound by rules that help push it in the right direction. Currently, this does not seem to be the case. There seems to be a misplaced distrust of government, whereas in reality the federal government has saved our society and our economy more than once since the start of this century. In 2008/09, the banking system and the financial system were saved from collapse. In 2020, the economy that was about to be strangled by tax liabilities was kick-started by federal government spending when $2500 checks were mailed to every American to get the economy going. Also, various acts by the Biden administration that increased government spending did increase private sector income, as every $ of government spending is a $ of income for US private companies and households. This is why the rate of unemployment came down so quickly. Economic policy executed by the federal government converted a US economy on the brink of collapse in the early stages of the pandemic into an economy where labor shortages appeared.

While many commentators think that this also led to a rise in the rate of inflation, by now most economists agree that the inflationary episode that started in 2021 has been due to a rebound in energy prices along with COVID-19-related supply side issues. The inflation rate in October 2023 was 3.2% in the US and more or less the same elsewhere. If an increase in government spending in the USA would have caused higher rates of inflation, US inflation should be higher than in the Eurozone, where government spending was roughly flat. In October 2023, inflation in the Eurozone stood at 2.9%, just 0.3% lower than in the US. If that is the price to pay for a full recovery of the economy, then it seems to be a great deal!

2.3 Government Spending, the Public Deficit, and Inflation

Most ideas about economic policy are simple—too simple. In order to think clearly about macroeconomic challenges, let us start with empirical observations.[26] First, we note that there is unemployment in the economy. Some of

---

[26] If you think that this is an obvious way to start, let me say that this is not what economists think. Their macroeconomic modeling mostly starts with assumptions about behavior and everything else follows.

it is involuntary unemployment—there are workers willing and able to work who cannot find a job. The reason is simply that there are not enough jobs. The tax liabilities have created more unemployed workers than the government has decided to hire. Since the government can always spend more money, we should think about a policy design that targets full employment. Otherwise, full employment will only result by coincidence. Another empirical observation is that consumer goods prices fluctuate, which means that the purchasing power of consumers is fluctuating as well. Just like unemployment, that is a bad thing. It would be preferable to have low and stable rates of inflation, though studies have shown that higher inflation itself doesn't seem to hurt real wealth or growth.

As it happens, a low and stable rate of inflation (price stability) as well as maximum employment are policy targets for the Fed. They are not policy targets of the federal government, and it is not clear why they are not. The federal government can create jobs by spending more money. If it buys goods and services from firms, it creates private sector jobs. If it hires workers directly, it creates public sector jobs. Why not do that until involuntary unemployment is effectively zero? One counter argument that is often brought forward is that government spending would be inflationary. Whether this is correct is a matter of spare capacity and the prices paid by the state. It is in the end an empirical question.

Figure 2.2 shows the data for government spending and inflation in the USA. Generally, there is no tight negative correlation. A rise in the growth of government total expenditures does not correlate with a rise in the inflation rate. This is most obvious during the pandemic, but also over the last four decades of the twentieth century. In the 1960s and 1970s, the growth in government spending was consistently higher than the inflation rate. Only in the early 2010s was the inflation rate higher than the growth in government spending. Oddly enough, government spending during that part of the Obama administration was falling and eventually turned negative, so one would expect a fall in inflation if the argument held any water—but it didn't.

As we can see, inflation did not seem to react to years and years of rising government expenditure. Even in 2020, a huge increase in government spending coincided with very little inflation. This only changed in 2021, when energy and primary product prices rebounded. The oil price was negative as late as in April 2020. In March 2022, it hit $100. Since consuming gas and energy is a core activity of our economy, the consumer price index increased—higher inflation resulted. Secondary effects started to show up as well, as energy is an input in fertilizer, thus affecting food prices across the board.

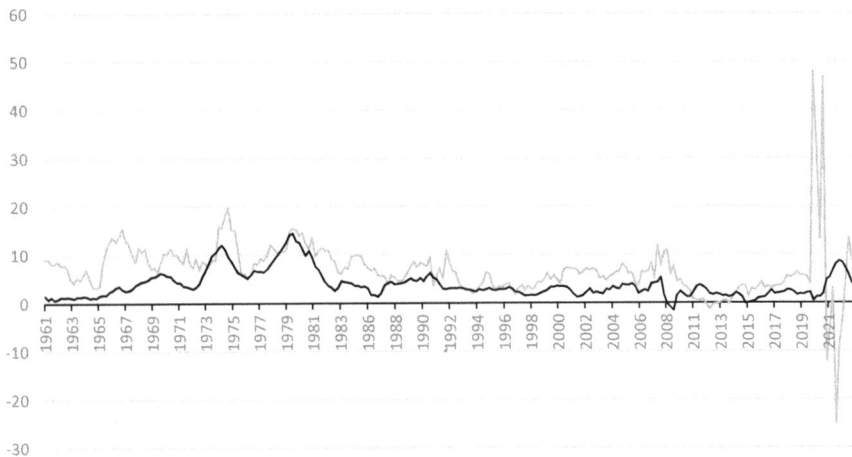

Fig. 2.2 Change in government total expenditures (gray) and rate of inflation (black), annual growth rate, quarterly data. *Sources* BEA [W068RC] and BLS [CPIAUCSL]

Once the inflation rate approached 10% in spring 2022, more and more firms increased prices regardless of increases in costs. The reason was simple: those firms increased their profits, hoping that consumers would accept higher prices. Given the price increases in many sectors, firms hoped that consumers would not be able to differentiate between firms that increased prices because of higher costs and firms that increased prices without an equivalent rise in costs. So, profits can also drive the inflation rate up, as Weber (2021, 2023) has shown.

To some extent, wages were part of the story as well. While most sectors saw wage increases fall behind the inflation rate, at the bottom of the income distribution results were a little bit different. For the 10% with the lowest incomes, wage increases outran price increases, leaving them better off. But that was not the general result—most workers have lost purchasing power.

The public deficit, which is the gap between government spending and tax revenues, does not seem to correlate with a high rate of inflation either. This should not be surprising. After all, a collapse of demand in the economy is what triggers a collapse in tax revenues and hence an increase in the public deficit. In times of economic crisis, the rate of inflation is low and this is reflected in the data, as Fig. 2.3 clearly shows.

Another idea debunked by Stephanie Kelton in her NY Times bestseller "The Deficit Myth" is that public deficits add to the public debt, which would then threaten our public finances. Bankruptcy would ensue, rather sooner than later. However, no such thing has ever happened. The Fed is the

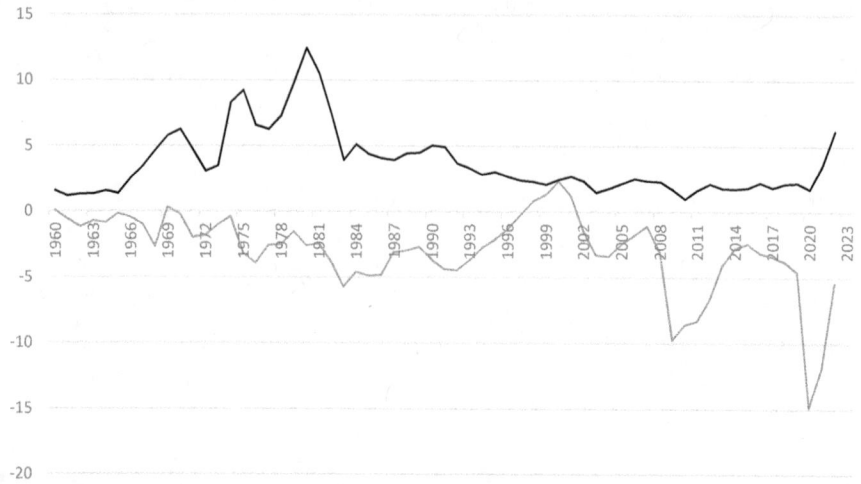

Fig. 2.3 Federal surplus or deficit in percent of GDP (gray) and rate of inflation (black) in percent, annual data. *Source* U.S. Office of Management and Budget [FYFSGDA188S] and BLS [CPILFESL]

monopoly supplier of US dollars, and the monetary rules are set up in a way that ensure that the federal government will not run out of money. So, we should not be afraid of public deficits or public debt. They are not necessarily per se inflationary, and they don't add "debt"—there is no such thing as the "public debt" that needs to be paid down all the way to zero. It is just a word that describes the nominal value of the money that the US government (at all levels) has spent minus what it has recovered in the form of tax revenues.

Therefore, monetary rules that allow us to target full employment and price stability should not build on the public deficit or the public debt. There is no economic case to be made that somehow restricting government spending is good for the economy because it creates more jobs or generates target inflation. A short look at Scandinavian countries confirms this. In countries like Sweden, government spending as a share of GDP is at about 50% compared to 23% in the US in the fiscal year 2022. Nevertheless, the inflation rate in Sweden is not higher than that of the US, and since the late 1990s its (Sweden's) unemployment rate is consistently higher. Also, Swedish crowns are expensive to buy in international markets. Apparently, even with a bigger government there comes no price to pay in the form of higher inflation or a loss of purchasing power regarding imports. The "price" Sweden pays is that it leaves less resources to the private sector to organize. But Swedish people seem to like the result because they could have voted for parties that want to cut government spending at any time.

Let us return to monetary policy and the consequences of higher interest rates. In the US, Silicon Valley Bank was the first victim of rising interest rates and their financial consequences, which in this case was a liquidity crisis due to a regulatory failure to restrict uninsured deposits.

2.4 Monetary Policy, Inflation, and Financial Instability[27]

Silicon Valley Bank was closed by state regulators on March 10, 2023. The reason was imminent over-indebtedness: it was feared that the sum of the bank's liabilities would exceed the amount of its assets. That fear resulted in a "bank run". Uninsured depositors panicked and tried to transfer $40 billion out of SVB on a Friday. SVB went to the Fed with collateral to borrow reserves that they would need to execute the payments, but it was half an hour late and so the bank failed. Let's take a closer look at what banks do and why some cease to exist.

A bank is an institution that performs credit analysis as a government agent. It buys from companies and households their respective promises to pay (redemption) with its own promises to pay in state currency (dollars, or euros), which we know under the name of "bank deposits". In contrast to the central bank, which holds a monopoly on state money creation (the Federal Reserve System), commercial banks can therefore only create "money" in the form of credit balances in state currency. This is also the reason why banks can go insolvent and central banks cannot. The latter can always put new money into circulation in the form of reserves. Banks, on the other hand, can only create money in the form of promises to pay. This money, however, is a liability from the banks' point of view.

Thus, when we (households) borrow from a bank, we are not borrowing money in the sense that we are borrowing existing money. Instead, after signing a loan agreement, the bank will increase the balance in the borrower's account. These are promises to pay, because the bank is, after all, promising that we will be able to make payments with our dollar balances. To do this, we can withdraw cash from the bank and make the payment ourselves, or the bank will handle the payment for us when we make a wire transfer. If the recipient is with the same bank, then the bank will increase their balance and

---

[27] This is a translation of a blog post published in German at https://www.dirk-ehnts.de/l/svb-uber-geldpolitik-und-bankenbeben/. The English translation will be published in the International Journal for Pluralism and Economics Education (IJPEE). I would like to thank Jack Reardon for help with the editing.

decrease ours. If this is not the case, the bank must go into settlement and either pay with reserves, offset payments, or postpone the payment into the future (loan).

So, in order to be able to implement the banks' promise to pay, they rely on a cash supply and use of the payment system—these are both provided by government institutions.[28] So, we hold that banks depend on the state at a fundamental level, and not the other way around. The state is the creator of money, having mostly delegated the monopoly of money creation to its central bank—the Fed, which debits/credits member bank reserve accounts on its books. Banks need reserves at the central bank both for settlement with other banks and for exchanging into cash. How do they get them? By selling financial assets, like government bonds, to the central bank (noting that lending is a subset of spending). The central bank declares what collateral it will accept. Thus, banks can borrow reserves from the central bank against a corresponding interest rate, or they sell government bonds to the central bank outright.

This view is far removed from the textbook view, where a central bank lends money to banks which then lend on to the private sector. This, though, is technically impossible, since households and firms do not have accounts at the central bank and hence cannot receive reserves. It is also technically impossible for banks to lend out saving (a flow of unspent income) or savings (stock of money wealth) as bank deposits are a liability for the bank and not an asset which it can lend out. Thus, textbook concepts like the money multiplier, fractional reserve banking, and banks as intermediaries to coordinate saving and investment are not describing operational reality.

In the real world, the central banks' most important tasks are to provide and maintain the payment system and to supply/sell/lend cash to the banking system. In addition, as the state's fiscal agent it makes payments on behalf of the federal government and acts as a lender of last resort to stabilize banks in a crisis. It acts as a dealer of last resort for government bonds to stabilize government bond prices and ensure that the government does not run out of money. Monetary policy as an instrument, on the other hand, is relatively new, and it is only in the last hundred years or so that central banks have been changing the interest rate in order to steer the economy.

A bank's survival constraint

A bank is granted a privilege by the state pertaining to the money creation facility—note that we are talking here about bank deposits in dollars and

---

[28] Banks use CHIPS, a private clearing system, to minimize the use of the payment system. See https://www.theclearinghouse.org/payment-systems/chips.

2 The Biden Administration and the Copernican Turn 23

not the dollar itself—which can be very profitable. After all, it allows banks to generate billions of dollars by lending to households and companies. (Whether this is actually value creation or value skimming is debatable.) The state wants banks to inject promises of payment via loans which are destroyed by repayment of the loan later. It would be unfair if some households or firms receive bank deposits that they do not (have to) repay. Second, inflation could result if banks constantly create more new bank deposits than are destroyed by repaying loans.

For these reasons, the state regulates banks. It imposes all sorts of conditions that they must meet before and while operating. One condition is that the value of all assets must exceed the value of all liabilities. The idea is that the bank should be solvent. It should be able to weather a storm. In other words, it should have positive equity (roughly: assets minus liabilities). So, if customers want to convert lots of bank deposits into cash, the bank can either buy cash outright, or borrow cash from the central bank against its assets, which it uses as collateral, and then satisfy the demand for cash. The central bank acts as a lender of last resort just when other banks are no longer lending reserves.

Silicon Valley Bank (SVB) was a somewhat special bank because it had quite a few clients from Silicon Valley. Companies there sometimes get a lot of money paid into their accounts, which they are required to keep in those accounts when they go public, or successfully complete a round of financing. This means that SVB always had significantly more bank deposits than loans. In balance sheet terms, this means that the SVB has loans to the private sector (households and companies) and some balances with the central bank (reserves) on the asset side and bank deposits and bank capital on the liability side. As long as the interest rates on loans and the interest on reserves are higher than the interest rate on bank deposits, everything is fine. In this case, the bank itself sets two of these three interest rates, namely the interest on loans and the interest on deposits. The interest rate on banks deposits is set by the bank, while the interest rate on deposits at the central bank (Federal Reserve Bank) is determined by monetary policy.

The low interest rates on deposits retained from clients' minimum balance requirements in the Corona pandemic prompted SVB to buy government (MTG) bonds at 3% with the zero-interest-bearing reserves, which are not subject to higher interest rates, which basically comports with the goal of (short term) profit maximization. However, interest rates rise with maturity, and in order to achieve significantly positive interest rates SVB had to buy government bonds with multi-year maturities. In 2020 and 2021, no one expected interest rates to rise in the future, which in turn wiped out

SVB when blind fear caused depositors to violate their agreements to keep compensating balances and incur substantial penalties and instead transfer them to other banks. Let us have a closer look.

The SVB purchased government bonds worth several billion dollars in recent years. This asset also appeared accordingly on the balance sheet, valued at market prices. Low-yield government bonds were relatively attractive in a low interest rate environment, and their price was therefore correspondingly high. But then the environment changed. The Fed raised its interest rate in response to rising inflation rates. As a result, interest rates on new government bonds also increased. This happens automatically because otherwise banks would stop buying government bonds. If banks are receiving interest on their reserves at the Fed at 4.65%, then a 10-year government bond with an interest rate of 3% becomes relatively unattractive. As government bonds trade, their price falls. Who would buy a government bond that pays 1.65% less interest than what the Fed pays? Only when the price of the government bond falls will it find buyers again. So, a ten-year government bond with a face value of $100 million will trade in the market for less than $100 million. The buyer not only gets the interest rate, but also a premium because she/he is not paying $100 million to redeem $100 million but only, say, $90 million.

In this way, all government bond prices fluctuate in price depending on the current interest rate. These price fluctuations are relevant in the market, but the owners of government bonds can ignore market prices and hold the government bonds until maturity and continue to earn a positive spread so long as clients' compensating balances remain. So, if you bought a government bond for $100 million with an interest rate of 3%, you will not realize a loss—you will get the money back plus the interest in the end. The market price simply expresses that the bond is relatively unattractive. But it is not necessarily a threat to a bank. The problem for banks like SVB is that they put the government bonds on the balance sheet at market prices ("mark-to-market"). This reduces the asset price, and thus the restriction that the value of the assets exceeds the value of the liabilities (positive equity) is harder to meet. SVB suffered a loss of $1.8 billion after it revalued its portfolio of government bonds. However, the compensating balances gained value equally, but regulation doesn't mark that value to market, so on paper the bank reported a loss.

SVB became a victim of rising interest rates, but there was risk not locking in a positive spread to the compensating balances on its books. Central banks use interest rate hikes as a standard tool to fight inflation. The official logic is that higher interest rates cause private investment projects to become unprofitable if the income from that investment doesn't also increase.[29] If less is then invested (built), first, demand for goods and services falls, and second, wage and price pressures abate (due to higher unemployment and less demand for goods and services). Both should cause inflation to fall. However, there are several problems with this logic.

First, many companies react to rising interest rates by raising their prices. Then, investment projects are still profitable and are carried out. When demand is strong, who wants to lose customers to the competition, which is also facing rising interest rates? In the real estate sector, do rising interest rates lead to falling prices in the short term? It depends whether real estate is financed or bought with savings. Why should rising interest rates make any difference? In addition to the problems described above, they also have an expansionary effect, since the government's interest payments to the holders of government bonds are now rising. They have reached about one trillion dollars in early 2024. If the recipients consume a positive fraction of their interest income, demand will rise.

Rising interest rates are currently causing government bond portfolios to depreciate. This will put institutions under financial pressure if their borrowing costs aren't also fixed, and bank regulation and supervision require banks to match the cost of funds with the returns and not take interest rate risk. Actually, this is not the point, at least officially, but if you take a look at history, before these regulations were put into place, you will see the start (not the development) of financial crises as a result of interest rate hikes.

The last major period of interest rate hikes was the 2000s, resulting in a real estate market crash followed by a global financial crisis. Before that, interest rate hikes in the late 1990s were followed by the dot-com crash. Superficially, interest rate hikes do not go away without financial collateral damage. Digging a little deeper however, other factors were responsible for those crashes, which both followed a large drop in government deficit spending and a spike in oil prices. So, the question is whether interest rate variation to fight inflation makes any sense at all. The data indicate that low interest rates (black) are not at all negatively correlated with high or rising inflation rates (gray): the highs are not correlated with the lows or falling ones. Interest rates and inflation rates thus correlate positively instead of negatively—the central banks' theory fails in a reality check (Fig. 2.4).

The collapse of SVB was the result of monetary policy, only in that it led to a panic among depositors who were willing to pay high penalty rates

---

[29] If possible, firms can raise prices so that the returns from an investment project increase in line with interest rates.

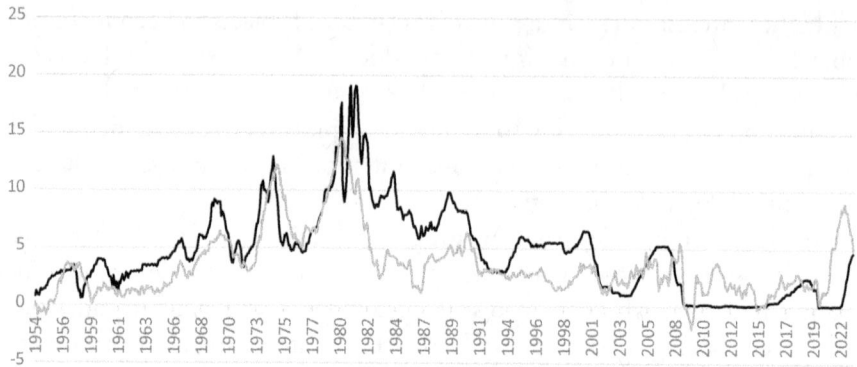

Fig. 2.4 Inflation rate (gray) and Fed funds rate (black). *Source* FRED (FEDFUNDS, CPIAUCSL)

to transfer their deposits to other banks. Some said it was predictable that banks would be hit and that other banks would follow, but none have since the initial panic and the Fed informally guaranteed uninsured deposits. Since the state protects all banks through deposit insurance anyway, the question at this point is whether interest rate hikes actually make any sense, given the resulting bank problems. Maybe monetary policy is not the right instrument? There must be better ways to deal with inflation. Currently (early 2024), inflation is down to 3% without any sign of the economy collapsing. This means that the whole monetary policy framework has failed to gain any traction. Larry Summers and his co-authors wrote last year: "In fact, fighting inflation will require a reduction in job vacancies and also an increase in unemployment".[30] But employment has been steadily rising since, and inflation has decreased (Fig. 2.5).

If inflation is not to be fought via an increase in bank failures, resulting from rising interest rates, then the state perhaps should issue a formal deposit guarantee covering deposits of all sizes. This would remove the non-economic incentive to withdraw bank deposits from SVB and other institutions. Or accounting rules could be adjusted so that government bonds are no longer priced "mark-to-market". The central bank could also accept government bonds at full payout value as collateral (no haircut), making it easier for banks to borrow reserves and avoid being forced to sell their currently low-priced portfolio of government bonds in the event of a bank run.

---

[30] Blanchard, O. A. Domash, and L. H. Summers (2022), Bad news for the Fed from the Beveridge space (July 13, 2022). Peterson Institute for International Economics Policy Brief 22-7, https://doi.org/10.2139/ssrn.4174601.

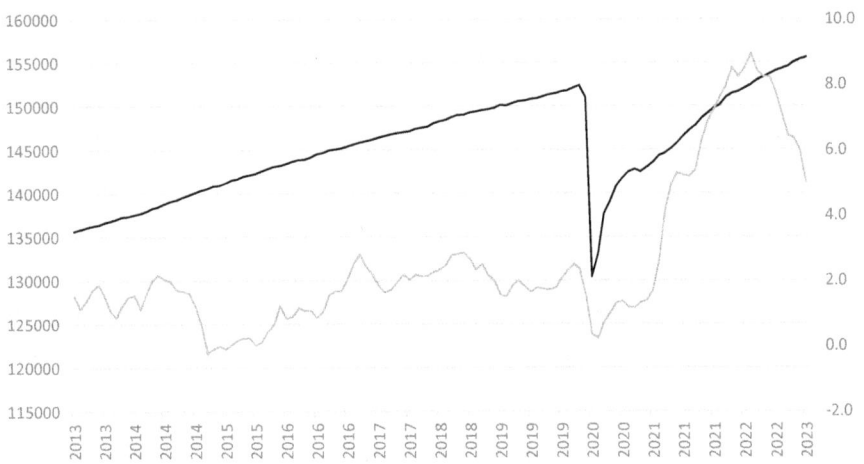

Fig. 2.5 Inflation rate in precent (gray) and employment in millions (black). *Source* FRED (PAYEMS, CPIAUCSL_PC1)

Alternatively, the government could only issue government bonds with a one-week maturity—or refrain from issuing government bonds altogether. This would simply allow banks to collect the deposit rate from the central bank; there would be no valuation of government bonds. Reserves are reserves; their value does not change with changing interest rates. Another solution could be to "park" the central bank's interest rate, which will be discussed in a later chapter.

SVB shows that we should rethink our monetary and fiscal policies for the twenty-first century. We still prefer monetary policy and private debt, even though fiscal policy and government debt proved to be the great savior in the pandemic. Recurring financial crises are the price we pay for our ignorance.[31] By keeping government spending at too low a level, permanent involuntary unemployment of millions of Americans results. This forces policymakers in Washington to think of ways to increase private investment to create more jobs, which is done by deregulating finance and pushing down interest rates, so that another bubble can be created. They also deregulate labor markets so that firms can hire at lower wages, or they can even hire and exploit under-age workers, which is on the rise.[32]

---

[31] Aliber, R Z., Kindleberger, C.P, and R. N. McCauley (2023), Manias, Panics and Crashes: A History of Financial Crises, Springer, Cham.
[32] Gerstein, T. (2023) "Are We Actually Arguing About Whether 14-Year-Olds Should Work in Meatpacking Plants?" New York Times, March 27, Opinion | Are We Actually Arguing About Whether 14-Year-Olds Should Work in Meatpacking Plants? Accessed June 26, 2023.

Since private investment is partly financed by an increase in debt, this way of running the economy always threatens to end in a financial crisis. While the federal government cannot run out of money, private firms and banks can and do. The business cycle is still with us. Any increase in total spending in the economy will lead to an increase in tax revenues because incomes will have increased. The resulting removal of purchasing power surely will lead to a lack of demand down the road—a recession usually results. Having the federal government spend more money would improve financial stability and move more resources into activities that maximize public purpose and private profit. In the USA, the Inflation Reduction Act is a case in point. The federal government spends dollars on subsidies to help private firms shift toward the production of electric cars and trucks. This is a win–win situation for the private and the public sector as well as for Americans.

The public needs to be educated that there is a choice. Increasing government spending is a viable policy option; and the European welfare state, including Scandinavia, clearly shows that there is no such thing as a "slippery slope" to socialism. The New Deal was politically successful, but it did not lift all boats and it created too much resource use. A new version should address climate change and sustainability as well as social issues and inequality. Government spending should not be limited by dogma or political rules like the debt ceiling or CUTGO, which are dysfunctional. Instead, the government should ask itself: what are the resources that we need to tackle the deficits of society? What are the opportunity costs (explained later) of using these resources? What would happen to the prices of these resources? The federal government should increase spending with an eye toward full employment and price stability while ensuring at all stages that resources are managed sustainably.

The discussion about the right economic policy that we should have had in the aftermath of the 2008–09 financial crisis is really just beginning. The polycrises that we are seeing now are the result of not having had that debate earlier.

3

The Paper Currency of Virginia (1760s) and Its Lessons

The current monetary system features two types of money. One is the deposits created by the US federal government and the Fed in the form of balances held by banks at the central bank (also called reserves or settlement balances) and cash. The other money is deposits created by commercial banks: bank deposits, which are promises of payment in state currency backed by the respective bank. The current monetary system is somewhat complicated because there are two monetary circuits. The first one centers on the Federal Reserve Bank, where the government and banks have accounts. Banks can clear payments among each other through the Fed, which also acts as a fiscal agent of the state, executing payments for governments at municipal, state, and federal government levels. While it can be explained how today's monetary system works, with all bells and whistles, it is quite time-consuming. Instead of filling fifty pages with balance sheets, institutions, and legal texts, I prefer to present a little story that is loosely based on historical evidence about how paper currency used to work in Virginia in the 1760s. The British colony in America and its use of money holds some lessons for the twenty-first century, I believe.

So, let's get into the boat, ready to go back in time to the year 1760. The declaration of independence is 16 years in the future, the French revolution 29 years away. We—a group of a hundred people—are on the Atlantic Ocean on our voyage to the promised land—there is no Statue of Liberty yet, but we would not know because we just decided to emigrate to the British colony of Virginia to start a new life, never having been to America before. We probably ran away from religious wars in Europe, suppression in Latin America or had some other very good reason to leave behind our loved ones, our homes, and our communities. We arrive in Virginia, more precisely on the Atlantic coast of the colony. To keep things simple, we take possession of an uninhabited island. The first thing we do is to determine who gets what land. In order to do that, we introduce a democratic system. The people get to elect a mayor. A simple majority is enough. After electing our mayor, the land is divided evenly. (That's probably why a majority voted for that candidate!).

Some citizens brought animals from their country of origin: cats and dogs, pigs and cows, goats and horses, and some chickens. We spend the first few months cultivating our land, creating pastures, orchards, and fields for cultivating crops. We spend time building tools that help us with agriculture, fishing, and hunting. We also build sheds, huts, and houses to provide us with shelter. It is quite a busy time, since we also take care of the elderly, children, and other citizens who cannot provide for themselves. After completing one year, we find out that we can survive on our little island—hooray!

Now it is time to take care of the children. It was nice to have them around for 12 months, and they became competent at all kinds of activities and skills, but there is agreement that a school would be best. The mayor suggests creating a public school and a road to ensure that the children can attend classes regardless of the weather. We all like the idea. Let's build our children a nice school and a nice road! Surely, the road will be used for other activities as well, business-related or else. And let's not forget that we need two teachers to put in that school. The mayor nods, then scratches his head. How can we build and operate this public infrastructure? The local government, located in a little office in the mayor's house, does not own any resources. Nor can the mayor command people to work. Since this is a small village, he gathers all citizens and asks them to help him.

A debate starts right away. What about having volunteers build the road? Not a bad idea, but when it comes to teachers we talk about full-time jobs. Also, we want to have infrastructure with good quality—and definitely not bad teachers. Ok, so what about forcing citizens to work for the government? Unacceptable, this is (or rather will be) the Land of the Free. But if we are all free and nobody cares about the public purpose, then how do we create what we want as a group? What about paying for everything, suggests somebody. Nice idea, but we did not bring any currency—we spent everything on the passage and the animals and things we brought here. Can't we create our own currency, the mayor wonders. The citizens start to murmur. Such monetary arrangements are used in other places, and some citizens have some experience with them. Some minutes pass, and the mayor is ultimately convinced that setting up our own currency would help us build the road and the school and hire two teachers. The state does not have resources, but we do. If the

3 The Paper Currency of Virginia (1760s) and Its Lessons

citizens would sell labor, land, goods, and services to the state for money, then our government could use those resources to get us what we want.

A monetary system is more elegant than the older solution of taxing people in kind. In many European regions at the time, the church took 10% of everything that was produced. Then, some goods were sold and others bought so that the church could come up with the resources it needed to run the church itself and other institutions. The drawback of such a system is that the church has a lot of buying and selling to do. It would only be by coincidence that the church acquired by taxation exactly what it needed in terms of resources. It is much better for the government to just buy what it needs. It feels like a fairer system of providing resources and probably is.

So, having settled on a monetary system instead of taxation in kind, the mayor takes out a pen and some paper. Being practically minded, his first question regards the units of currency. What should it be? The answer to that one is easy. As a British colony, the currency should be named "Virginia pound". Pound sterling was the currency of the motherland, where George III just started his long reign (1760–1820). Since no traders visit our little island (yet), we leave the question of the exchange rate for later. The question whether our currency would be backed by gold is a definitive no. We do not have any gold nor can we make promises to convert our currency to gold (coins) or other precious metals. The mayor decides to continue with our plan anyway.

The next question regards the quantity of Virginia pounds that would be paid for one day of construction work at the road and the school. Also, a wage must be established for the teachers. Would a fair daily wage be one pound, ten pounds, or a hundred pounds? In order to answer that question, we would need to know the prices of consumptions goods: a sack of barley, a gallon of milk, an ox, or a box of apples. However, no prices exist yet since nothing has been sold for money so far. Only when money would first be paid out through the government—spending it on labor and goods—would prices be established. It is only logical that the price should roughly correspond to the amount of labor that was necessary to produce any good or service. So, the choice of the nominal wage would be rather insignificant. If the mayor pays a low wage per day, then prices would be low—and if the mayor pays a high wage per day, then prices would be high!

It seems that the purchasing power does not depend on how much money we pay for labor. What will be offered for money at what prices we simply don't know—but we'll find out soon enough! If we bartered goods already, relative prices are roughly known anyway. If one hour of road work can be "paid" with a dozen apples, then surely the price of an apple will be the twelfth part of one hour of road work. How many apples would be on offer is a good question. Anyway, the mayor declares that the wage rate will be one pound per day for road work and one pound per half a day of teaching to reward the advanced knowledge and skills of the teachers, which surely took time (and resources) to acquire. Since there are twenty shillings to the pound, an apple would probably be priced at 1.67 (=20/12) shillings. But let's not get ahead of ourselves.

So, the mayor declares, now that we know how much money to spend, let's look for that money. We need five pounds each for the road worker and the construction worker for the first week, which makes ten pounds. How do we get ten pounds? Silence. The citizens scratch their heads once again. Then, Mr. Samuel speaks up: we can collect taxes in our currency. The mayor thinks about this hard. "How are we going to collect taxes in Virginia pound if the citizens do not have any money?", he finally asks. So, the tax proposal is off the table. (For now—we will see later why the government taxes us. Spoiler: it is not to "finance" the government.) The government has to spend first, before taxes can be collected. Mr. Samuel does not give up easily: "We could sell government bonds!" Again, our mayor is not convinced: "Our citizens have no money to buy government bonds with either", he says. The government has to spend before citizens can buy government bonds. Mr. Samuel surrenders: "Ok, let's just print the money and get it over with. I'll do it myself". As a skilled printer, he is the best pick for that operation and the mayor is glad that this question is settled.

After a quick debate with those artistically inclined, a design is found and Mr. Samuel retires to his little house to get the printing press going. After the lunch break, the citizen assembly resumes its meeting. Mr. Samuel is back, proudly showing around the ten pounds worth of "notes" (there is no bank!). So, the mayor says after thanking him for his effort (at the end of the month, he will be paid one pound for every hundred banknotes he prints, by the way), let's get to it. Who wants to work on the road or school next week in return for a pay of five pounds? The citizens first look around, then look at their shoes. Nobody says anything. The mayor is not pleased. Apparently, it is easy to print money, but it is hard to get it accepted![1]

---

[1] Inspired by the late economist Hyman Minsky, who came up with that phrase.

3 The Paper Currency of Virginia (1760s) and Its Lessons

3.1 Provisioning the State and Money Printing

Creating a demand for money is easy. The government can impose tax liabilities on its citizens. While Virginia originally used a poll tax, payable at elections, we assume here that the mayor imposes a tax by law which is payable per head. Each citizen between 18 and 65 has to pay a certain sum at the end of the year in Virginia pounds. Citizens who do not pay taxes when approached by the tax man will be sent to prison. A police officer is needed to ensure that this law is enforced. In this way, the mayor ensures that state currency is accepted by the citizens. It is demanded by those that need to pay taxes. Taxing citizens creates sellers of labor, goods, and services, as this is what citizens can do to acquire the money they need to pay taxes—and stay out of prison. Taxes are not created so that the government will have money. It already has money, but it does not have resources. So, the government uses money to provision itself.[2]

The "real" tax is the amount of time given up by the citizens, both when working directly for the state and when working on the production of goods and services that are subsequently sold to the government. The modern monetary system is just like the old system of paying taxes in kind. In the Middle Ages, citizens were often required to give up 10% of their production to their landlord or the church or both. This transfer of resources provisioned the "government", which usually was not democratic. Taxes had nothing to do with "financing" the government—it was just a way to transfer resources from citizens to the "state". If the government used up the resources for itself, then citizens were poorer as the result. Revolutions were not uncommon when the people perceived that their resources were being wasted.

Interestingly, the monetary system as displayed here starts with the imposition of tax liabilities to create a demand for money and, at the same time, to create sellers of labor, goods, and services. The monetary system does not somehow evolve from a market, where buyers and sellers find it convenient to use a currency instead of, say, gold coins. While there are dozens of examples of tax-driven (paper) currency systems, there is not a single description by an historian or anthropologist showing how money evolved out of the marketplace. Modern money is what we use to pay our taxes and make payments to the state. It is the currency which the state has organized as its monopoly, having full control over the quantity that is issued. (That does not mean that the state sets the quantity of money, for instance defined as the sum of all cash or reserves—in modern times, this is left to central banks and they

---

[2] This is inspired by Warren Mosler, who first came up with that phrase.

often supply what is demanded to ensure that the banking system has enough liquidity.)

Returning to the mayor's monetary operations, the next question is: what should be the amount of tax liability per citizen? To answer that question, the mayor should look at what he is planning to purchase this year. A road and a school are to be built, two teachers hired—that requires Virginia pounds to be paid and labor to be offered on behalf of the citizens. If the mayor does not tax at all, the (100) citizens will not provide any labor. If he taxes one Virginia pound per head, he will get 100 days of road-building work or 50 days of teaching or any combination of the two. So, the mayor sits down and thinks about his projects. To build a road and a school will take 150 days, and the school will be open 200 days a year. This means that the mayor will pay 150 Virginia pounds to construction workers and £400 to teachers. In total, 550 Virginia pounds will be spent.

Should that be all, then, the mayor asks? Well, a concerned citizen answers, some of us might want to save some money so that we can work less next year. Also, we like to build up wealth in the form of money because other citizens will offer us goods and services for money. Could you maybe spend a little bit more to allow us to save some money? Ok, says the mayor, what about an extra 50 Virginia pounds so that total spending will be £600? The citizens nod in agreement. "You could also lower the tax so that we can keep some of our income", a younger citizen suggests. The mayor agrees with this idea. I will tax you at 50 Virginia pounds per head. Since total government spending will be £600 but tax revenues only £500, there will be £100 in extra saving (unspent income) for citizens. Who the savers will be depends on your preferences. Those who like to consume now will not do a lot of saving, and those that prefer to spend later (next year) will do some saving.[3]

The mayor asks the citizens once more if they would be willing to work on the road and the school and now, he finds a taker. About £5 is paid out to two citizens who accept the job offered by the government. Effectively, the government has turned these two citizens into "workers", a new class of citizens that work for a nominal money wage! Imposing tax liabilities creates a demand for money and a supply of "work" (as well as goods and services offered to the government). Paid work logically has to appear after money was introduced, but we see here that the connection is much tighter than normally assumed. The same goes for unemployment. Before the mayor imposed tax liabilities on the citizens, there had been no unemployment. Citizens were working, engaged in agriculture, child care, gardening,

---

[3] Saving is unspent income over a time period, whereas savings is a stock of wealth. It is easy to confuse the two concepts.

3 The Paper Currency of Virginia (1760s) and Its Lessons

fishing, and all kinds of other activities, but these were not paid with money wages. Some citizens were poor and others rich—the introduction of money does not necessarily change that.

Nevertheless, the mayor needs to make sure that everyone can find a job or else there will be citizens sent to prison because they cannot pay their taxes. Employment is the direct consequence of government spending. It does not matter whether the mayor buys something from a private company or hires a worker directly—employment goes up when the government spends. There is functionally only little difference between the government employing public workers and spending money on goods and services or giving it to citizens to spend (which is called a transfer). The effect on employment is most direct when the government hires. When it buys from firms these might run down stockpiles and not increase production. However, when the government buys continually from firms, they will and do increase production—if not, the government will surely find other sellers!

The government can also decide to pay out £ (pounds) as a transfer of income. This should also increase employment as the receivers of this income will probably spend at least a part of it. The increase in demand for goods and services will make firms expand production, which means buying more machines (capital or investment goods) and hiring more workers. The share of income that citizens spend varies with total income. Those having low incomes usually spend almost everything as they face many pressing needs. Those with high incomes already can afford everything they need and more and might save all the additional income they earn. One example would be the stimulus checks sent by the Biden administration. Some used that money to buy consumer goods and pay the rent, and others used it to gamble in the stock market or pay their taxes. The latter probably reduce their supply of work or goods and services that they sell for dollars. (This, by the way, is why Universal Basic Income (UBI) might create economic problems—it reduces the number of sellers of work, goods and services in the economy. As a result, prices might be more volatile and generally higher than they are now.)

The government has the power to reduce involuntary unemployment to zero. Some citizens will be voluntarily unemployed, as they are waiting for their job contract to begin, prefer to stay at home and take care of the elderly or children, or have another good reason not to work. Involuntary unemployment consists of citizens that would like to work and are able to work, but cannot find employment to pay taxes or save. This is not the situation in our village in Virginia, where the mayor had drafted the budget with a view to full employment. Now, imagine a new mayor comes in, being elected on a platform of "fiscal responsibility" (which is quite the opposite, as we will find out soon). He cuts government spending in half so that out of a hundred citizens, only fifty are employed. About twentyfive are directly employed by the government, spending part of their income on consumption so that twenty-five workers are employed in the private sector. All workers are saving a part of their income to pay taxes later and to have some money left at the end of the year. It is the unspent income that is the problem. This means that fifty are unemployed and looking for a job! How do we cure the unemployment problem?

One solution might be to train the unemployed workers. Let them learn new skills and languages, gain new knowledge, and improve their organizing. However, this won't work. There are only fifty jobs. In order for unemployment to fall, somebody needs to spend more money! Either the fifty workers spend a part of their income or the government spends more. Since it is not the task of the workers to bring about full employment—a situation with zero involuntary unemployment—it is the government's responsibility to increase spending accordingly. Only with higher spending will we see unemployment fall, given everything else.

A federal government's budget is thus crucial for employment. Injections of government spending create income for households and firms, which together constitute the private sector. A part of private income is spent on consumer goods. Those firms receiving that income will need to spend money to produce more, creating another round of spending—and so on. Also, firms distribute profits to households, leading to another increase in income. The logic of employment works like that: total spending in the economy determines total output, since firms sell for money. Total output determines employment, since goods and services are produced using workers. Therefore, total spending in the economy determines employment. It is assumed that working hours and technology (productivity) are fixed. In the long run, more can be produced by increasing working hours or productivity or both. That can only happen, though, if there is enough spending and hence enough demand for the additional output. Otherwise, firms would produce more output that they cannot sell, which means financial trouble. Unsold inventory does not translate into monetary income, which means that firms will have problems making payments at some point.

Total spending in the economy will only settle at a level that will bring about full employment by coincidence. For the last half century, total spending was not enough to reach full employment—not in the US and not in most other industrial countries. This means that the economy does not regulate itself. It does not come with an inbuilt "thermostat" that gives us full employment as if we are running the economy on autopilot. That's because unemployment starts with the implementation of tax liabilities that induce "fiscal drag". Subsequent government spending fills in the hole created by the tax liabilities. Tax liabilities place an uncertain drag on the economy as savings desires can fluctuate. The full employment response is to use net government spending to target full employment and, because there might still be some unemployment left, to offer jobs to anyone willing and able to work, which lets "markets" determine the indifference levels of savings desires.

This is why economic policy matters. With economic policy, we get instruments that we can use to hit economic goals. The traditional two goals followed by a newer one are:

- Full employment.
- Price stability.
- Sustainable resource use.

We have already defined full employment. Price stability is another goal, meaning that prices of consumer goods should be stable over time. That does not mean that consumer goods prices are constant over time—the usual definition of price stability is to allow prices to increase by 2% per year. How can we help the mayor in our Virginia village to bring about price stability? One idea would be to increase all the prices that the government pays by 2% every year. This includes wages paid to public employees. If these have an income that grows by 2% every year, they can afford to pay higher prices. The mayor might also determine some prices himself. Maybe there is a public swimming pool or a horse cart that provides public transport services. The prices of these services can be increased by 2% each year to help with price stability.

If the government increases wages by 2% every year, the private sector will have to follow. Wages in private firms should also rise at 2%, otherwise the firms will have trouble attracting the best workers (if the government is hiring open ended). Since wages are costs from the perspective of firms, it makes sense them to increase prices accordingly. Hence, higher wages help to increase the price level so that it hits the inflation target. Higher wages also mean that companies have a reason to economize on the use of labor. Since they know that wages will only go up in the future, they have an incentive to use more machines and less workers. This leads to rising productivity and, in the long run, to shorter working hours and more leisure time.

The rise in productivity depends on the supply side. In some sectors, an increase in output will increase costs. In other sectors, an increase in output will lower costs. Most industrial sectors exhibit this kind of increasing returns to scale. The more machines and tools are used with an increase in output, the cheaper average costs will be. Why? Because the fixed costs of capital are divided by more units of output. The use of more tools and machines might also bring about a higher specialization of labor. This was the theme of Adam Smith, who argued (in 1776!) that the use of more and more capital will lead to more and more specialization of labor and thus to higher productivity. The "Wealth of Nations" was enlarged by the increase in output of consumer goods. A side effect of this is that with lower average costs prices will go down and not up. This helps with price stability.

If productivity growth is positive, wages need to grow faster. Why? Otherwise, firms will produce last year's output with less workers. That's a good thing. However, the wages paid out by firms would not be enough to purchase the whole output at last year's prices. That creates room for lower taxes or more public services. So, nominal wage growth has to reflect productivity growth. It would be a good idea to let wages grow at roughly productivity growth plus the inflation target. We should expect prices to be roughly stable, given that other prices in the economy—like energy prices—do not misbehave by gyrating wildly. Since in our village we do not use energy, it would be great if the mayor could announce that wages in the public sector will rise by 2% every year. This also helps firms to deal with an uncertain future. Now, they have information about the evolution of a strategically important price—the wage.

So, one policy designed to bring about price stability consists in wage-setting by the government and, as single supplier of needed tax credits, the government has no choice but to set a price. Since it affects government spending, we can subsume it under the rubric of "fiscal policy". We have already seen that fiscal policy has an effect on employment. It is quite likely that there is a spillover effect to price stability. At full employment, private firms would have to offer higher wages in order to attract additional workers. They would have to match the wage increases in the public sector. If, however, there is unemployment, firms might choose from a big pool of unemployed workers. There would be no need to offer higher wages as the unemployed workers would be desperate to take any job offered to them. To some extent, the existence of strong unions could mitigate this problem. Strong unions would force the firms to increase wages or face labor unrest. So, the distribution of power matters for price stability.

In the background there is a distributional struggle. For firms, wages are always costs. For workers, wages are income.[4] Whereas firms try to reduce

---

[4] Workers might have other sources of income, too, but wages are usually the most important one.

3 The Paper Currency of Virginia (1760s) and Its Lessons

wages to the lowest possible level, workers want to maximize wages. The interests of the firms do not coincide with the interests of the workers. Sure, some firms offer relatively high wages in order to attract the best workers. But that is not what the majority of firms do. They want lower wages, just as they want lower costs in other areas. The problem at the economy level is that lower wages lead to less spending on goods and services. Thus, if all firms are successful in lowering wages, they will find that they will not be able to sell their output at the prices they have set. They would have to lower their price (or let it grow more slowly) as wage costs are falling (or rising more slowly). This constitutes a fallacy of composition. What is good for one firm (lower wages, translating into higher profits) is bad if all the firms do it (translating into lower profits). Lower wages at the economy level translate into unsold inventory. Firms will not have higher profits and are forced to cut output and/or reduce prices.

Therefore, it makes sense to manage total spending in the economy. Keeping aggregate demand for goods and services high and stable is one goal of economic policy. One way to achieve this is to adjust government spending and tax revenues so that in good times spending grows more slowly and in bad times more quickly. The government can offer unemployment insurance and social security to ensure that a downturn in the economy does not lead into a downward spiral. The danger is that lower spending leads to lower output and hence to lower employment. The rise in unemployment would again lead to lower spending—a vicious circle results. If the unemployed were paid unemployment insurance and social security, demand would be stabilized. Also, social security contributions shave off some income in good times. Having demand grow more slowly in good times also helps with the overall target of stabilizing the economy. The government could additionally offer a job to everyone who can and wants to work but cannot find a job. This is called a Job Guarantee. (There will be more details on this later.)

So far, we have looked at the government's instruments when it comes to price stability. But what about monetary policy? In our little village in Virginia, there is no central bank. There are no banks either. Without interest rates at the mayor's disposal, monetary policy as used today is out of the question. Back in the 1760s, the government of Virginia did sell bonds, but they paid no interest. It was just a more convenient way of holding monetary wealth. The sale of bonds was definitely not about financing the government. Citizens returned some of the cash paid out by the government to the government in return for a bond that was nothing but a promise of payment of ... cash! Bond sales change the portfolio of the public, which consists of cash and bonds. Bond sales reduce the amount of cash in the possession of the private sector. However, cash that returns to the government does not constitute "wealth".

A Virginia pound is nothing else but an I.O.U. (I owe you), a tax credit. The government owes the holder of cash the acceptance of said cash for payments to the government. That is the only legal promise that is maintained. Since the government cannot make payments to itself, cash it possesses does not have any "value". It is the same with private I.O.U.s. Assume a villager pays for a bag of oranges with an I.O.U. worth five Virginia pounds. A week later, someone offers the issuer of the I.O.U. to give back the I.O.U. in return for a sheep. When the transaction is accepted, the sheep changes owner and the I.O.U. returns to the issuer. It would not be correct to say that this means that issuer is five Virginia pounds better off now—he clearly isn't. He could always produce new I.O.U.s as long as they are accepted. This is why a government cannot "save" in its own currency. It can always print more cash (or create digital money) and buy goods and services if it so desires. It does not have to recycle old cash.

3.2 Tax Revenues Are not "Financing" the Government

So why does the government collect tax revenues and bond revenues then? As we have already seen, tax liabilities drive the currency, which is why it is important that the citizens pay their taxes with Virginia pounds. (In our age, taxes as a driver of currency are not as important anymore as there is a lot of private debt which forces people to offer work for money. They have to repay their mortgage or real estate loan.) Tax revenues also reduce the purchasing power in the hands of the citizens. If the government wants to spend, it is easier if people have less money. There is less competition for the resources that the government wants to buy. The government can proceed more easily with its plan to increase prices for everything it buys by 2% as firms often find that the government is the only buyer. If there would be additional buyers offering to pay higher prices, firms would sell to these.

The tax system should be set up in a way to stabilize demand as well. If tax rates increase with nominal income, the relative amount of purchasing power that is withdrawn when the price level increases grows. This works at the firm level as well as at the household level. For firms, tax revenues are a function of the price, and for households, tax revenues are a function of the wage. This constitutes another automatic stabilizer. One could also tax consumption directly, withdrawing purchasing power with every sale of goods and services. This is what the sales tax does. Of course, one could also tax land and wealth in progressive ways so that an increase in the price level would increase tax revenues there. Because distribution matters, finding the best taxes and tax rates is a political and therefore highly complicated issue. There is no reason for taxing the rich in order to give the money to the poor—this kind of romantic idea belongs to a gold coin economy. If there is a social issue that needs to be fixed, our mayor can always address it by printing more money, given that the resources that are needed are available. Only if the resources are already used new and/or higher taxes would be needed.

While we will not go into the details here, in a modern economy tax revenues and bond revenues drain reserves (central bank deposits held by banks) and thus keep the interest rate stable that banks charge other banks for borrowing reserves. Since there was no Treasury and no central bank in Virginia in the 1760s, we'll discuss this issue later. We will also go into the details of modern monetary policy and how changes of the interest rate are supposed to change the rate of inflation.

There is still one economic policy target to discuss: sustainable resource use. Goods and services are produced using resources of all sorts: raw materials, energy, labor, machines, land, and much more. If we want to continue producing in the future what we are producing today, we must ensure that production is sustainable in the sense that resources are used in a way that allows them to be used in the future as well. Some resources can be grown and never depleted. Others are mined and depleted. The biggest issue of all is energy use. Burning fossil fuels—coal, gas, and oil—is the main cause of global warming. Climate change is already happening, as many areas on planet Earth are now warmer than they were a century ago. Since back in the 1760s this issue was not relevant, the discussion will be shifted to later chapters.

So, let us resume with our look at the economy of that little village in Virginia. The mayor just spent ten Virginia pounds to pay construction workers. He has done that because the mayor cannot possibly do all that work alone. So, the government has to provision itself, and the monetary system is its instrument to do just that. The workers are working for the government voluntarily. If they don't want to work for the government, they could work for a household or firm that pays out money. Citizens need the cash for the tax payments at the end of the year. The tax liabilities have been forced on them by the government (in the person of the mayor), which represents society as a whole. Spending public money ensures that our citizens get the public schools and public roads which they can use for free. There is no need to introduce a toll or a fee to put children into school. The government can spend money and promote the public purpose without being forced to be profitable. That does not mean that it should waste resources. Since these are limited, the government should ensure that they are managed well.

Now that £s have entered the monetary circuit, we can also start looking at economic statistics. Gross domestic product (GDP) is the sum of all expenditures. By definition, GDP equals the sum of consumption goods purchases, investment goods purchases, government spending, and exports minus imports. Government spending is £10 currently, so GDP is £10 as well. What about the public deficit? The public deficit is defined as government spending minus tax revenues. Since taxes will be paid only at the end of the year, tax revenues are still zero. This means that the government's deficit is £10: it spent £10 more than it taxed! Note that there is no problem with the mayor running out of Virginia pounds. As long as there is paper, ink, a printer, and political will, more £ can be produced on demand. There is no issue of insolvency since the government is the currency issuer. As such, it might solve and create many problems—running out of money is not one of them. Of course, political rules can be instituted that would prohibit the mayor from spending more money, but these are just that—political rules. The federal government does not run out of money, but it can lose access to money.

A public deficit of £10 does not sound threatening, but if we look at the public deficit to GDP ratio we arrive at 100%! That surely must be a bad thing, right? Whether it is a bad thing depends on our economic goals. Do we have full employment yet? No. We need to spend more. Is there price stability? Yes. And there are still lots of idle resources that government spending can activate at the going price. Since the mayor cannot run out of money either, there seems to be no problem with a deficit to GDP ratio of 100%. Quite the opposite: the private sector (households and firms) has financial saving(s) of 100% of GDP![5]

Every £ spent by the government increases public debt £ by £—but it also increases monetary saving by the non-government sector since income is rising without a rise in expenditure (which might happen later). So, government spending leaves the private sector financially richer! It owns ten £ now which is unspent income (so far). From our perspective, it is not a public deficit, but private financial saving. Both of these concepts—deficit and saving—are flow concepts, meaning that they occur over a period of time. We can move to stocks by adding flows to the stock of the last period. "Public

---

[5] Saving is the income not spent, and they build up the stock of savings over time. At the very start of the monetary system, and only in the first year, we start from zero savings, so that saving equals savings.

debt", for instance, equals the "public debt" of last year (it was £0) plus this year's public deficit (£10 so far). Therefore, "public debt" currently stands at £10. This corresponds with financial savings—now with the "s" added at the end it is a stock—of the same amount. The government spends some £ but did not promise to "repay its debt". So, what is the "public debt"?

The "public debt" is the money spent by the federal government that has not been used yet to pay taxes. That's all there is to it. It is a statistic. It does not make any sense to call it the "public debt" since there is no promise of repayment. The "public debt" cannot be "paid" or "repaid" by the government. An increase in government spending will increase the "public debt" in the short term, and an increase in tax revenues will reduce it. It is as simple as that. A reduction of "public debt" would mean that more taxes would have to be paid by the private sector. There is no other way. Cutting government spending does not reduce the "public debt". Quite the opposite, it might reduce tax revenues even more! Even the International Monetary Fund thinks that a reduction in government spending will lead to more "public debt" and not less.[6]

3.3 Drafting a Federal Budget

We have learned from this episode that the mayor should plan his spending with economic targets in sight. It does not make sense to use fiscal statistics as policy targets. Public debt to GDP, the fiscal deficit—using these statistics as policy targets might lead to optimal policy, but only by coincidence. It would not be a surprise if we realized that the government might seriously underinvest in our future when it targets deficit and debt instead of the public purpose. Drafting a government budget is a completely different thing from drafting a household or firm budget. Those who do not understand that, even though they only mean it well, pose a danger to our society.

Whereas the currency user—the state/local government, firm or the household—does have to repay the money it borrowed, the currency issuer does not have to do any such thing. Simply because it does not "borrow" in the first place. It spends currency into existence that it later takes out of circulation through tax and bond revenues. Citizens can use their money to buy bonds, but these are only a promise of more money later. The government will "repay" the principal and interest of these financial instruments, but it will not repay the outstanding debt at once to bring public debt down

---

[6] https://www.imf.org/en/Blogs/Articles/2023/04/10/how-to-tackle-soaring-public-debt.

to zero. For a currency user, costs are costs in money. First money needs to be available, either through an income or through borrowing. Only then can the economic unit spend. The government at the state and municipal level also works like this. They need to tax and borrow before spending.[7] The federal government, as in the case of the mayor, can spend money and does not and cannot "finance"—it does not spend money they earned before.

Certainly, there are limits to government spending. The logic works like this. The federal government pays by creating money. Money then is not a limit. Resources are limited—labor, goods and services, land and capital as well as energy and raw materials that are offered for sale. What is also limited is what the government can buy for its currency. Some households and firms might not be selling everything to the government, so this restriction should be tighter. The mayor can only buy what the citizens are offering. If they don't offer enough, the mayor can decide to pay higher prices or increase tax liabilities, forcing people to offer more. Paying higher prices might reduce the purchases by the government though because sellers reach their target income more quickly and might decide not to sell more.

Just because the mayor can move resources into the public sector does not mean he should. In the background there is an economic and political calculation. Since resources can only be used once, the government should think about the value that these resources have to citizens if left to the private sector. Firms could use labor to produce more (consumer) goods and services, for instance. This means that the government should reduce its bureaucracy to a level where things are managed effectively. Otherwise, the workers could be used in the production of consumption goods, ensuring a higher "Wealth of Nations" (Adam Smith). This concept of looking at alternative uses of resources is what economists call "opportunity costs". It lies at the center of economics, which is often said to deal with "scarcity".[8]

So, how many resources should the government use? Well, that depends. In some countries, government spending accounts for more than half of GDP. These are the Scandinavian countries, with public health care, public trains, and a lot of other public goods and services that are run by the government and the public sector. If citizens are not happy with the allocation of resources, they can always vote for a party that promises "lean government" (a concept from the 1980s). After all, it is a political decision whether government should be big or small. In a democracy, the voters should have the final say. They should know that the government can pay for things just as private

---

[7] They also have to have a balanced budget, the law says.

[8] Economics is about much more than scarcity. Money matter, for instance, and also the understanding of how human beings and communities thrive and what motivates their decisions.

3 The Paper Currency of Virginia (1760s) and Its Lessons   45

companies can pay for things. While companies can borrow money from banks that they need to repay—hence the need to have profits—the government can spend its own money and not care about profits. In reality, there is always a mixture of these two ways of organizing resources. Ideologies of the twentieth century argued in favor of state-planning only (Communism) or market-planning only (Neoliberalism). Both these ideologies have failed. In the twenty-first century, we need to structure our institutions in a way that the public and the private sector work together. In our Virginia village this is not yet clear, since there is hardly any technology and infrastructure is basic (a road and a school).

Resuming our example, we have two construction workers with five Virginia pounds each. They probably expect to work some more for the government, so they are willing to spend some fraction of their income. Let's assume that they buy apples from a farmer for one pound each. Then they eat those apples. The ultimate goal of the economy is the consumption of goods and services, so this is good. Consumption has increased from zero to two pounds, as has GDP. What about the monetary side? The money now moves through the society. We call this the monetary circuit. Money is spent and spent again until it leaves the circuit. How? The only way that money can be destroyed is through tax and bond revenues. In Virginia, it is mostly tax revenues that destroy £.[9] So, payments among the private sector economic units redistribute income in the form of £, and only payments to the mayor destroy £.

The monetary system is a huge and important tool to organize economic activity. The state uses money to provision itself, and firms and households offer goods and services as well as labor and other things to get their hands on money. Whether the economic system works well is a good question—for whom, one might add. Everything is political as money is created by the law, which is determined through politics. There are no economic laws to speak of.[10] One can set up a monetary system this way or that way. If the people don't like the way the monetary system is run, they'll turn into unhappy citizens. At some point, they might openly revolt against the monetary system and the political system. This is what happened to the American colony of Virginia, which in the 1760s was in the possession of the British Empire.

In the eighteenth century, the British Empire was often at war with France. There was the Seven Years' War (1756–1763), which pitted the British and

---

[9] In Virginia during that time, tax revenues were burned. It was more efficient than transporting piles of cash through the colony. Bonds carried no interest rate and were a convenient way of holding large monetary savings.
[10] Well, spending causes an income of the same amount, but this is trivial and not a "law".

its allies against France and her allies. There was the French and Indian War (1754–1763), with the same parties fighting each other in North America. This meant that many resources were shifted into production for the war. There were less consumption goods available because of this shift and the British population did not like that. So, the British government came up with an idea. It would source some resources from its American colonies in order to increase consumption in the UK. Instead of ordering the American colonies to directly surrender foodstuffs, tobacco, and other goods, the British taxed the colonies—in pound sterling. The official story was that the public debt of the UK had doubled, so the British Parliament moved to impose additional taxes. However, it was probably the resource transfer that mattered more.

The Sugar Act of 1764 and Stamp Act of 1765 imposed taxes on sugar and anything printed in the colonies and the Revenue Act of 1767 imposed taxes on tea, among other things. At around the same time, with the Currency Act of 1764, local colonial currencies were outlawed. This meant that the American colonies had to completely restructure their economies. The government would lose its status as creator of currency and henceforth have to pay for all its expenditures just like everybody else (except the British government). In order to pay taxes to the UK, goods would have to be sold to (mostly British) merchants in possession of pound sterling. In return for the outflow of goods the colonies received pound sterling, which they needed to make the tax payment.

What resulted was a massive outflow of resources that impoverished a large share of the American population. At the same time, the colonial government was not allowed to print new money and spend. These changes in the way the monetary system was set up helped to bring about the American Revolution in 1776. American colonists opined that there should be "no taxation without representation", which became a slogan. What is missing from many historical accounts is the fact that the taxes had to be paid in pound sterling. The subsequent reconfiguration of the American economy to export goods to the UK, with local governments being unable to organize resources because of the prohibition on money printing, was probably the main economic reason for the American Revolution.[11]

Summing up, currency should be seen as a public monopoly. The government uses money to provision itself—it wants our resources. It does not want our money, even though we think that this is what taxation is about. Ultimately, the government uses the monetary system to ensure that it can do its job. It hires labor, pays for goods and services, pays rent and electricity bills,

---

[11] https://history.state.gov/milestones/1750-1775/parliamentary-taxation.

and builds and runs infrastructure. The government will not use all the available resources, since that would leave no resources in the hands of the private sector. Since resources can be used only once, the government needs to think twice before buying something from households or firms. If the resources can be put to use in a better way in the private sector, the government should not purchase them. The private sector can be innovative and dynamic, and in some sectors, it has been proven that resource management is best left to the private sector. This does not mean that the federal government is not innovative and dynamic—after all, they put two men on the moon.

Ultimately, the government decides which parts of the economy will be organized by the public sector and the private sector respectively. It is a matter of degree. Nobody would argue that all resources would have to be managed by the state or that all resources would have to be managed by the private sector. The paper currency of Virginia helps us to better understand the monetary system from the perspective of the currency issuer. Things are more complicated today, since we have a digital currency. Households and firms hold bank deposits in the banking system, whereas banks hold deposits at the central bank. This setup is more complicated that the paper currency of Virginia, yet most results and the intuition concerning the currency issuer do carry over to the modern world.

4

Modern Money Theory as Part of Economics

MMT did not reinvent the world, but rather borrows—mostly unconsciously—from older economic theories or arrives at the same conclusions. For example, the German economist Georg Friedrich Knapp, who wrote the book "State Theory of Money" in 1905, was unknown to Warren Mosler, although Knapp's book begins with the sentence[1]:

> Money is a creature of law; ….

Knapp had understood that paper money issued by the state flows back to the state from the taxpayer and that gold or other metals would not be conceptually necessary for the money function.[2] This, incidentally, distinguishes him from Karl Marx, who wrote in Volume 1 of Das Kapital (own translation): "This is only state paper money with a fixed price in terms of gold. It grows directly out of metallic circulation itself".[3] This theory of money is not compatible with MMT, in which state money is not a consequence of metallic circulation.

Statements by other economists have been adapted for the purposes of MMT as a kit of ideas (eclectic empiricism) after their ideas were rediscovered. These include, for example, Joseph Schumpeter's idea of creative

---

[1] See Knapp (1924, 1).
[2] Knapp notes at the bottom of the first page of his book that is not in favor of "unbacked" paper money.
[3] See Marx (1914, 85).

destruction in dynamic capitalism and John Maynard Keynes' theory of effective demand as a driver of economic development.[4] Other theories, which MMT revives and complements in parts, concern the purely functional view of government spending according to Abba Lerner ("functional finance") or Hyman Minsky's insight that the fluctuations of the business cycle are based on financial cycles and the investment activity of private firms. Thus, capitalism would be necessarily unstable and require stabilization through government economic policy.[5] All these theories are the subject of this book. The term theory is defined by the German dictionary Duden as follows (own translation):

> system of scientifically founded statements explaining certain facts or phenomena and the legalities underlying them.

As a theory of money, MMT deals with facts and phenomena of the monetary system:

- Who can create money?
- How is money created?
- What are the money circuits?
- How do they interact?
- What explains involuntary unemployment?
- Who determines the level of interest rate(s)?
- What explains inflation?
- How can goals such as full employment, price stability, and sustainable resource utilization be achieved?
- What is the role of the government in economic policy?

The lens that MMT provides builds on the use of accounting, specifically double-entry book-keeping (Ehnts 2019). Both at the microlevel (households, firms, banks, central bank, treasury) and at the macrolevel (all households and firms, the government sector, the rest of the world), balance sheets are used to record money flows. The findings based on this method are rooted in logic. For example, if the government sector runs a surplus because tax revenues exceed government spending, then the non-government sector (households, firms, and the rest of the world) must run a corresponding deficit. After all, they have transferred more money to the government than they have received in the form of government spending. The surplus of the

---

[4] See Schumpeter (2021) [1912] and Keynes (1936).
[5] See Lerner (1943, 38–51) and Minsky (2008).

government corresponds to a deficit of the others—and that includes us, as households.

Such insights are based on pure accounting. If we add a bit of behavior (which is always subject to uncertainty), we can use it to build macroeconomic models:

Macroeconomics = Accounting + Behavior

If, for example, a country's imports depend on consumption, which in turn depends on wages, then it is relatively easy to show where export surpluses could come from: from the evolution of wage. If wage growth at home is weaker than abroad, then imports will not rise as fast as exports (which depend on wage growth abroad). This only serves as a first example to explain the method of accounting. We will return to the conclusions of MMT regarding foreign trade later.

MMT and economics today

If you want to study MMT in more detail, the only places to do so today are Bard College in upstate New York and the University of Missouri in Kansas City (UMKC) in the US and the online study program "Economics of Sustainability" offered by Torrens University. In Europe, there is only the possibility to participate in the MMT Summer School in Poznań (Poland) or in my course at the Maastricht Summer School (The Netherlands).

Since MMT is "only" a theory of money, it is connectable in all directions. For example, anyone who deals with the planetary boundaries of economic activity, like Raworth (2017), should also understand money. Otherwise, fatal errors could creep into economic policy recommendations if, for example, it is assumed that money is also limited and not available in the desired amount. This could lead to the misconception that we cannot afford a socio-ecological transformation because we would not have enough money. So, unfortunately, financing would not be possible—which is, of course, nonsense. Unfortunately, myths like the deficit myth (see Stephanie Kelton's brilliant book) or the taxpayer money myth have been propagated for decades and have painted a skewed picture of reality. In this respect, MMT can contribute to enlighten citizens and policy makers and enable a social and ecological transformation.

Also, very much in line with MMT is Mariana Mazzucato with her theories of the role of the state.[6] If the state can spend money as needed and only the resources (labor, land, energy, etc., that are offered to it for its money)

---

[6] See Mazzucato (2021).

limit its activity, what does targeting the public purpose as envisioned by MMT look like in practice? What are the roles of private and public sector? To what extent should the state also think and act as a business? How do we get government employees or officials to take on risks? How do we create an equitable distribution of risk between the state and private companies? All these questions are eminently important for our polity, but looking at balance sheets alone does not answer them.

MMT explains how money works. Once this is understood, further questions can be raised that are of high relevance for societies. In this respect, MMT is suitable as a starting point to branch out into questions of social science. MMT is not a theory that has answers to all questions, nor will it ever be. However, a modernized economics can be built around MMT and based on *homo socio-oeconomicus* instead of the rational individual, namely the individual embedded in social structures.[7] The problem of scarcity, which currently dominates economics, would thus fade into the background. Instead of maximizing utility through consumption and gross domestic product (GDP), alternative policy targets including full employment, price stability, and sustainable resource use would move to the forefront.

4.1 The Failing Monetary Policy of Inflation Targeting

The central bank controls interest rates, not the quantity of money. The main policy question is at what level the central bank should set interest rates. The basic ideas of the currently practiced monetary policy of inflation-targeting are relatively simple and are explained in the following sentences. The level of the inflation rate is seen as essentially determined by the change in unit labor costs (costs of labor per unit of output). These are determined by the changes in productivity and wages. If wages grow faster than productivity, then the money in the worker's wallet will grow faster than the cake it buys. Enterprises realize that the demand for pieces of cake is greater than the supply and increase the price of a piece of cake. When this is reflected in the consumer price index, we have a higher inflation rate as a result.

The central bank can now try to influence the wage growth rate by changing interest rates. In doing so, the central bank assumes that an increase in interest rates will cause banks to raise interest rates in turn. Given the demand for bank loans, this should lead to a reduction in the quantity of

---

[7] In Ehnts and Jochem (2020) we sketched out some thoughts about how to redevelop economics.

credit, because at higher interest rates some investments would be no longer profitable. Lower investment would lead to higher unemployment, less wage pressure, and consequently to weaker demand for goods and services. The inflation rate would fall. Conversely, if interest rates are lowered inflation should rise as more investment projects are now realized, which increases wage and price pressures.

(Private) investment and interest rates

In reality, however, a negative correlation between the key interest rate and private investment cannot be found. Higher interest rates lead to higher interest payments on government bonds and thus increase the income of the private sector, adding to aggregate demand since a part of that additional income will surely be spent on goods and services. What the effect on private investment is nobody knows for sure. Perhaps it depends on the overall fiscal stance. If the federal government is increasing government spending, demand for goods and services as well as for real estate might go up. We would expect an increase in private investment to follow as firms expand production to meet the additional demand, and this is what we have seen in the US in the last years. In other countries, where public debt is lower and real estate is financed by long-term loans with variable interest rates, private investment might fall and overcompensate any positive demand impulse from the fiscal stance. There is consensus that not much happens when interest rates are reduced. If a company's production is limited by a lack of demand for their goods and services, even a zero interest rate will not convince them to expand output capacity.

Figure 4.1 shows that gross private sector investment as a share in GDP has fluctuated relatively little over the past half century. In the 1990s, it was still above 20% of GDP; since 2000 it has been below 20%. Central bank interest rates went up in the 1970s (not shown), then down since the 1980s. Around 2000, the main refinancing rate was 3%; at the time of writing (November 2023), it is 5.25–5.5%. Despite this, there has been no significant decrease in private investment in recent quarters. The idea that the interest rate influences the share of private investment in GDP does not reflect reality.

Some reasons for this failure are obvious. Companies only increase investment if they believe they will be able to sell the additional production. Demand therefore plays a major role for companies. Zero interest rates do not encourage companies to invest more, because they realize that demand is not rising. We have probably been in this situation for most of the years in the 2010s.

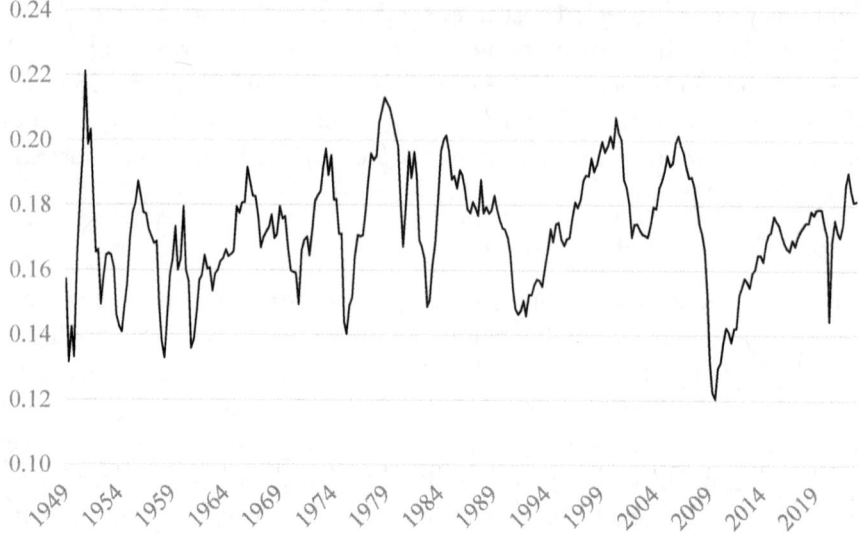

Fig. 4.1 Share of gross capital investment in GDP, 1949–2022. *Source* U.S. Bureau of Economic Analysis (A006RC)

This means that (expansionary) monetary policy is not working: lower and zero interest rates and bond purchases are not driving the inflation rate up. The explanation is simple: the Fed creates additional central bank money through quantitative easing (QE) and bond purchases, but the banks cannot lend it on to households and companies. We do not have accounts with the central bank. From a technical point of view, the banks cannot pass on the balances at the Fed to us. The simple reason is that the banks cannot enter an account number for the recipient as we do not have an account in the payment system. One solution to the problems would be for the government to make more money available directly to companies and households. They might not have to pay the money back, as with stimulus checks or subsidies. This brings us to fiscal policy. Whereas monetary policy is about lending money, fiscal policy is about spending money without any provision for repayment.

4.2 Government Spending

As the creator of money, the state has a privileged role. It is the only actor in the economy that need not finance (and actually cannot) its expenditures and can thus spend regardless of the level of its revenues.[8] It does this through its central bank. The latter pays the federal government's bills by marking up the respective balance of the account of the receiving banks accordingly, always on behalf of the Treasury. Since these "increases" in account balances are, from a technical point of view, independent of any other changes, government payments are only linked to the central bank.

Politically there may well be barriers. For example, a central bank might have a rule that there must be a sufficient balance in the government's account before transfers can be made on behalf of the government—like in the US. The money is ultimately created within the political process, when the federal budget is passed. What is contains may and can be paid for by the federal government. Any other result would be extremely disappointing from a democratic point of view. What good is democracy if our government is restricted in its spending? What if the central bank refused to spend? This has never happened in the entire history of the US. As the fiscal agent of the state, the central bank has an obligation to the federal government to provide it with appropriate financial resources.

The independence of the central bank

The central bank is usually independent of politics in the sense that it conducts day-to-day business without political intervention. However, independence is often misunderstood as a broad freedom to act on its own and even to supervise the government. However, the Federal Reserve Bank is not and never has been endowed with such a mandate. As part of the state, it is also the subject of legislative amdendments, i.e., politicians can change the laws regarding the Federal Reserve Bank. Conversely, the central bank cannot change the laws regarding the federal government. The central bank usually ensures the solvency of the federal government. It does this by promising to buy government bonds in case of doubts, so that investors are convinced that they always have a buyer up their sleeve. Under this institutional arrangement, government bonds are de facto risk-free. This is common practice at almost all central banks in the world.

---

[8] Note that in can only spend on things that are part of the budget. There has never been, there is no, and there never will be "unlimited" government spending. Those who warn against this have no clue about how the political process actually works.

The Eurozone, where twenty European countries share a supra-national currency, tried to follow a different path. When tax revenues in Greece collapsed during the euro crisis in the early 2010s, the European Central Bank (ECB) refused to ensure the country's solvency by buying Greek government bonds. With the low tax revenues not being enough to refill its account, the only alternative source for deposits at the central bank was cut off. The Greek government officially ran out of money because its central bank denied it access, following the Eurozone rules. A partial debt default (a so-called haircut) followed. The Greek central bank was able to create euros during all this time, but it was not allowed to do that anymore on behalf of the Greek government because its balance was negative. The episode caused economic suffering, unemployment rose, production fell, and savings in the form of government bonds devalued. The Greek economy has not recovered from the shock to this day. Even before the coronavirus pandemic, Greece's GDP had not reached its 2007 pre-crisis level.

With the *Pandemic Emergency Purchase Program* (PEPP) created in March 2020 and replaced by the Transmission Protection Instrument (TPI) in July 2022, the ECB is breaking new ground in this crisis. National governments are supported, which has stabilized their government bond prices and prevented a second euro crisis. This program should be seen as a step toward normality, with the ECB coming of age and finally using the "superpowers" that other central banks have long been using. The lesson from Europe is that the central bank can always ensure that a government can spend. It is a political, not a technical question.

Money as a tax credit

Modern money, which is always issued by a state institution, helps the government to appropriate the resources it needs to do its job. In doing so, the state should have the public purpose in mind and not use the resources in the interest of a few. Whereas some centuries ago the state was entitled to 10% of everything that was produced (the so-called tithe), today it intervenes purposefully via the monetary system and appropriates only those resources which it needs. This use of a monetary tax is much more efficient than taxation in the form of goods.

From our perspective as users of currency, modern money works as a tax credit. The state does not promise a peg to gold or other currencies (unless it fixes an exchange rate), nor does it promise any other redeemability outside the payment of taxes. Thus, modern money is what we use to pay our taxes and make other payments to the state. Because we know that we and others will have to pay taxes in dollars in the future, we accept our state's money.

What matters to us is not only its value (purchasing power), but the demand for currency that forces us and others to accept dollars in exchange for the supply of goods or labor.

The taxpayer myth

Taxes are therefore not a means of "financing the state" at the federal level. There are very different reasons for levying taxes. On the one hand, they reduce the purchasing power of companies and households. This is very practical when the state wants to spend more money, because it frees up resources that would otherwise have been taken by the private sector. Money can command resources, and those with less money command fewer resources. Therefore, taxes can be used, among other things, to release resources that the government can buy at given prices. Otherwise, it would have had to bid up prices and wages in a bidding competition with firms and households. In addition to reducing inflation, taxes can also serve to protect democracy from exorbitantly high wealth, which implies corresponding power for its owners. Or they reduce the consumption of goods that are considered harmful, such as alcohol and tobacco.

The idea of government spending being put on the shoulders of "taxpayers", on the other hand, does not correspond to reality. The money our federal government spends does not come from taxpayers. The money is released through the federal budget and created by the central bank. Even if the federal government replenishes its central bank account with tax revenues as well as proceeds from government bond sales—this is not central bank money nor does it "pay for" spending. It is a kind of score, because the government cannot hold wealth in the form of tax credits—the government does not make payments to itself, as we have seen. Tax credits in the hands of the government are not tax credits just as cinema tickets in the hands of the management of the cinema are not cinema tickets. So, as long as the Fed ensures that the federal government can sell its government bonds, there is no reason to believe that tax revenues have any effect on federal government spending. Only political rules like the debt ceiling, debt brakes or deficit limits can create this effect artificially.

The "excuse" put forward by national politicians that the higher spending during the crisis was only possible because savings had been made beforehand as a result of low fiscal deficits or even surpluses are factually incorrect. Our monetary system simply does not work that way—the state is not like a household who has to save before it spends!

Unfortunately, reports that "taxpayers" paid for the bank bailouts, the policies required to support the economy after the financial crisis of 2008/

09 (which was a real estate boom and bust), and so much more are still widespread. It is the other way around: the "taxpayers" are the ones who depend on the payments of the state. Without income in dollar, there would be no tax payments in dollar. And the state is a large player whose expenditures triggers both a large amount of income and tax payments. The federal government's spending is ultimately "paid for" by the Fed's money creation, because it creates the reserves which are used to buy Treasury bonds, and so it is our public money. There is no taxpayer money, there is only public money.

Consequently, government spending at the federal level is not limited by tax revenues. The amount of government spending is determined by the federal government's budget. This is a political and not a technical limit (at least as long as the debt ceiling is no problem). It is an essential part of the democratic form of government that Congress, with the representatives of the people, takes the decisions on what and how much money is spent. Anyone who disagrees must accept the accusation of going against democracy.

So: Let's say goodbye to the taxpayer myth—it's our money! Who saved the banks with their money? We did. Who saved the economy after the lockdowns in 2020 with their money? We did. Who paid for the welfare state? We did. (Who will pay for the Green New Deal? We will.)

4.3 Government Bonds

Government bonds were pieces of paper issued by the government that pay out interest on and a certain amount of money (principal) when they mature.[9] As we have seen, these bonds are not used to fund the federal government.[10] Government bonds are interest-bearing tax credits (except Treasury Bills, which are short-term paper).[11] They establish a risk-free interest rate on which banks can base their lending. If investors can buy a risk-free government bond with a fixed interest rate of, say, 4%, they will

---

[9] For many years now, government bonds have been digital entries in a book-keeping system in most countries, including the USA.

[10] All these operations have the Fed buying Treasury bonds from banks, paying by crediting their accounts. Open market operations are executed to influence the interest rate(s) in the interbank market, and QE is thought to influence bond yields over all maturities and asset purchase programs.

[11] Technically, they are called Treasury securities. Five different varieties exist: Treasury Bills, Treasury Notes, Treasury Bonds, Treasury Inflation-Protected Securities (TIPS), and Floating Rate Notes (FRNs).

certainly not lend their reserves to other banks and financial market participants at an interest rate of less than 4%.[12] There would always be a risk that they would not get their money back. So, the interest rate on government bonds for the different maturities set a floor. Government bond sales to the public reduce the liquid assets in the hands of the private sector and can therefore act as an incentive to save, which reduces demand.

The federal government of the US, through the New York Federal Reserve Bank, sells its government bonds exclusively to the primary dealers, a group of banks in the so-called primary market. In contrast to the secondary market, where "used" bonds are sold, only new bonds are sold here. This is analogous to the purchase of new cars at a car dealership and the used car trade, where used cars can be bought by anyone.[13] The banks do not pay for the government bonds with their own bank deposits, because that would make payments for the Treasury extremely complicated—it would have to manage more than 20 different bank accounts. Also, it would lose money if one of these banks would go bankrupt. Instead, the primary dealers (the banks) pay with reserves from their respective accounts at the Fed.

These reserves must therefore exist *before* the government bonds are purchased. The Fed ensures that the banks have sufficient reserves when the government bonds are sold. The state, to which the central bank belongs, must logically first issue money before banks can use it to buy government bonds. This shell game only obscures the fact that it is ultimately the Fed that enables government spending by providing reserves to the primary dealers.[14]

The Fed also acts as fiscal agent of the state.[15] This makes it clear that states do not need financial markets to make payments. They rely on the central bank to make payments. Everything that follows has nothing to do with financing government spending. Historically, bond issuance helped central banks to ensure that their fiscal function did not interfere with their monetary function. Here is an example. Imagine that the government spends a

---

[12] Note that reserves can be used to buy government bonds, but not to make loans to the private sector since they do not have an account at the Fed and hence cannot technically receive the money. This would change with central bank digital currency in the form of central bank accounts for everyone.

[13] Obviously, by now everyone can order a car directly from the manufacturer over the internet.

[14] If the banks have problems getting the reserves needed to buy the government bonds, the Fed will help them. In 2020, during the COVID-19 pandemic, the Primary Dealer Credit Facility was created to help the federal government sell more government bonds. Credit extended to primary dealers under this facility could be collateralized by a broad range of investment grade debt securities, including commercial paper and municipal bonds, and a broad range of equity securities, the Fed stated.

[15] Donna A. DeCorleto & Theresa A. Trimble, 2004. "Federal Reserve Banks as fiscal agents and depositories of the United States in a changing financial environment", Federal Reserve Bulletin, Board of Governors of the Federal Reserve System (U.S.), vol. 90, pp. 435–446.

billion dollars by having the Fed mark up the accounts of the receiving banks, which in turn mark up the accounts of their clients (firms and households) who are paid by the government. All the banks will have more reserves, and given that households and firms don't want to hold more cash (at least not a billion dollars), there is no matching increase in demand for reserves. So, when banks are trying to lend out the additional billion dollars in reserves to other banks they will find that there is not enough demand.

Their next step is to lower the interest rate and see if there is any demand then. Banks do that until they reach the interest rate on reserve balances, which outside the US is usually called the deposit rate—the interest rate they get from the central bank for doing nothing with the additional reserves. Hence, an injection of reserves through government spending drives the interest rate down to the deposit rate. Before 2011, the Fed did not pay interest on reserve balances. So, at least theoretically, before 2011 an injection of money caused by government spending threatened to drive the interest rate to zero.

That is why legislation was moved forward so the Treasury issues government bonds that mop up the "excess liquidity" created by additional government spending. In our example, the billion dollars' worth of reserves would be drained from the interbank market through the sale of a billion dollars' worth of government bonds. How would the Treasury ensure that banks would actually buy those bonds? The interest rate was the incentive for banks to buy government bonds. This allowed them to make higher profits because there was no interest rate on reserves. Historically, bond issuance is an interest rate stabilization scheme that allows the Fed to be both the fiscal agent of the state and the banker of the banks at the same time, without any interference. The Fed can make payments on behalf of the government and lend to banks at the same time, setting the interest rates on all maturities if it so chose. If it sets only some short-term interest rates, arbitrage determines the long-term interest rates and bond prices (and hence yields).

The monetary system of the USA was designed and redesigned with a purpose in mind. It is not some kind of "neutral" technology, but a political institution created by federal law. Money has never been "neutral" and never will be.[16] A democracy, for instance, can only work if the government has the right to draft a budget and spend money. Being elected by the citizens, it executes the will of the people. No institution should get in the way. If the voters don't like the way the federal government spends money, or thinks that it spends too much/little, they can vote for a different party and thus bring in

---

[16] See Eich (2022) and Feinig (2022) for books on money from a political science perspective.

a new government. Since the Fed has been created by law, it can be changed by law (if there is a good reason). A federal government is more powerful than the Fed because it can change the Fed, whereas the Fed cannot change the government. This is just a statement that describes reality and not a call to end the "independence" of the Fed, which should not mean more than the Fed's power to set the interest rate free from political interference but is often used in a much wider way.[17]

After the Great Financial Crisis of 2008/09, there was some talk about allowing direct monetary financing of the government (Turner 2015). This would allow the US government to sell bonds directly to the Fed. However, one could also think about a monetary system where the federal government runs an intra-day deficit at the central bank, similar to "overdrawing" its account (like in the Eurozone). Or, one might choose a system where the central bank makes payments on behalf of the government and no bonds are issued at all. In the UK in 2020, the British government was allowed to overdraw its Ways & Means account up to a limit set by the Bank of England.[18]

When the Bank of England would make a payment on behalf of the government, it would simply credit the account of the receiving bank. The additional central bank money then ends up in the deposit facility and earns interest accordingly. The British government never used this arrangement, but it was available. The banks are happy receiving interest. It is the same interest they would get from holding government bonds. In this respect, it is a myth that the government borrows money from (international) financial markets, China's government or from banks via loans or from the rich. The same is true for the other countries.

The Federal Reserve Bank is the only institution that is allowed to create US dollar.[19] So, all scarcity of money is political. Money can always be politically directed to where it is needed. Currently, most societies are allowing a lot of money to be created by commercial banks. We also allow a lot of credit to be created in financial markets and the real estate market. Aside from the pandemic years, we did not allow a lot of spending for the democratically legitimized federal government. It is a political decision whether we want the government—at federal, state or local level—or the private sector to use more resources in order to provide us with a combination of public and

---

[17] See Binder and Spindel (2017).
[18] See https://www.bankofengland.co.uk/news/2020/april/hmt-and-boe-announce-temporary-extension-to-ways-and-means-facility.
[19] Technically, it buys the coins from the Treasury. The Treasury is not allowed to mint coins and use them to pay for goods and services or anything else.

private goods. We should not be ideologically blind and call for all resources to be managed by private markets or by the government.

Some commentators claim that without the pressure on public finances governments would not be willing to reform. In my view, this is not supported by reality. With their own currencies and without any pressure from rating agencies, banks, financial markets, and speculators, the countries of Western Europe expanded their welfare states in the postwar period and came to grips with the problems of distribution and mass unemployment. With the rise of inflation-targeting and the use of monetary policy in the 1980s, problems of distribution and mass unemployment returned. This is not a surprise, since the idea of monetary policy is to use banks to finance more private investment in order to create employment. The dark sides of this policy choice are the shareholder orientation, which puts profits above public purpose (and everything else) and the rise in private financial debts, which create financial instability. While capitalist expansion is necessary for the economy to innovate, both the collapse of the New Economy in 2001–02 and the Great Financial Crisis of 2008–09 indicate that the size of the private sector has been too big. Some of the resources should have been allocated by the government. We could have had more, better, and greener infrastructure in the US by now. Well, too late for that, but not too late to learn from policy mistakes of the past.

"Government debt"—a smokescreen

If taxes and government bonds do not finance government spending, then "public debt" is something very different from debt of a household or a business. "Public debt" is inappropriate as a word when the government is the creator of the currency and as such can always put new money into circulation. The central bank is the fiscal agent of the state and protects it from an inability to pay. No other institution has this advantage. Therefore, we should not talk about "public debt", but about the outstanding amount of tax credits held by the private sector. The government has promised nothing in return except acceptance for tax payments in the future. The size of the public debt is determined by the money that the governments (at all levels) spent into the economy minus what has returned through tax payments. In other words, public deficits (government spending minus tax revenues) accumulate to form the "public debt", which is just a number.

An example will illustrate the difference between private and public debts. Suppose a household takes out a loan of $10,000. The money is spent and then income equal to the loan amount plus interest has to be earned. When the household has the money, it can pay off the loan and thus get rid of its debt. The federal government, on the other hand, generates its debt not through a loan, but through its spending, which exceeds its tax revenues. Let us assume that it spends an additional $10 billion. In doing so, the state promises nothing other than to accept these $10 billion in the future for tax payments or other payments to the state. It does not strive to reduce its debt all the way back to zero.

The state reduces its "public debt" when we pay our taxes! So, the state does not have to do anything at all to pay its "debts". It cannot pay them, but we pay our tax debts, and this is how the state gets back its own money. Anyone who demands that the national debt should be reduced must explain who should make higher tax payments to the state and why that would not cause the economy to collapse as some citizens will be poorer.[20]

Government spending and full employment

Government spending leads to more employment and higher aggregate demand. Since from a functional point of view spending can always be increased and the cost of generating more money is virtually zero, it arguably makes sense to use the federal government to stabilize the economy. If companies and households do not spend enough money to achieve full employment, the government can and should spend more money to achieve full employment. It can buy products from companies, hire more employees in the public sector, or ensure that all those who are looking for work find it by means of a Job Guarantee (right to work; more on this later.) Full employment is defined as the situation in which everyone who wants to work and can work has a job. Alternatively, the state can reduce working hours and thus redistribute work.

The state is responsible for unemployment. The cause of unemployment is not that some people are too unproductive, but that there are simply not enough jobs. The solution to the problem therefore lies not in the skills and qualifications of the unemployed (though it is never a bad idea to upgrade skills and qualifications), but in the creation of the necessary jobs. Additional government spending, like any other spending, creates additional jobs.[21] In addition, this also leads to higher incomes for households and companies. It is also reflected in private saving, the excess of income over expenditure in the private sector, and in their accumulation, wealth. Government spending

---

[20] The obvious solution here is to tax the rich, if one would be serious about it. The rich can also be taxed because their wealth is a danger to the functioning of democracy, as many billionaires use their money to buy political influence. John D. Rockefeller, who was the first billionaire, used to philanthropy to "correct" his public image. See https://blogs.loc.gov/inside_adams/2020/01/rockefeller-billionaire/.

[21] Lower saving rates would achieve the same goal but are hard to reach.

creates private saving, dollar for dollar. These two variables do not grow independently of one another. A reduction in government debt is only possible through a reduction in private assets, because this would be the consequence of increased tax payments or reduced government spending.

Full employment and Price Stability

Figure 4.2 shows that full employment and price stability are goals that have usually not been achieved together. While inflation in the 1960s was very low, the unemployment rate hovered around 5%. An increase in government spending probably would have led to more employment without increasing inflation, but it was not tried. In the 1970s, the two oil crises led to higher rates of inflation. Unemployment went up as well, causing a new word to be born: stagflation, the simultaneous occurrence of *stag*nation and in*flation*. After that, the inflation rate stabilized as the oil shocks were overcome by switching from oil power to gas and nuclear power and by reducing the power of unions, which lead to meager wage growth and is one of the main causes for the high income and wealth inequality that we see today.

Even the recent reduction in unemployment since 2005 has not been accompanied by rising inflation rates. In this respect, it is important to note at this point that an increase in employment does not in principle lead to more inflation! The 1970s wage-price spiral created by this struggle over distribution was ultimately ended by the USA shifting from oil to gas. The high interest rates of the Volcker era played only a minor part in these dynamics, whereas the reduction of the power of the trade unions was a real factor.

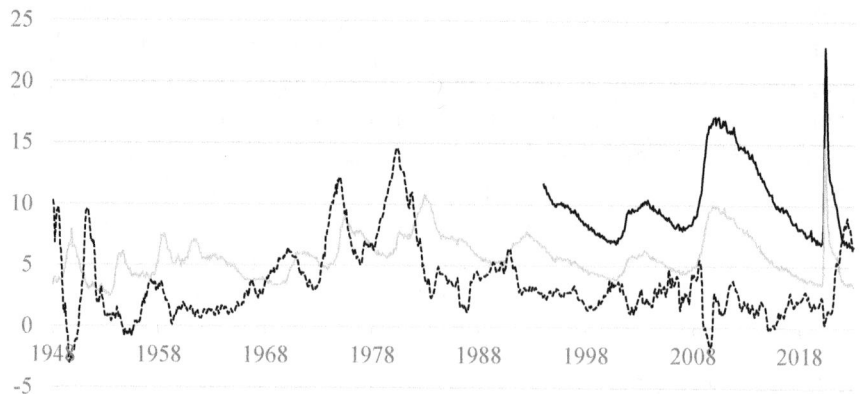

Fig. 4.2 Broad unemployment rate (U6; black), narrow unemployment rate (gray), and inflation (dotted), 1949–2022. *Source* U.S. Bureau of Labor Statistics (LNS13327709, LNS14000000) and FRED (CPIAUCSL)

Public debt and distribution

If the distribution of income or wealth is a problem in society, it can be alleviated by an appropriate distribution policy. Those who want to eliminate inequality should use the economic policy levers (e.g., tax rates and financial market regulation) and curtail the power of the rich. Interest rates on government bonds have not been a major driver of inequality. After all, they have been falling to zero since the early 1980s while inequality was steadily rising.

Full employment and price stability are compatible with an equitable distribution of income and wealth, as the postwar period partly has shown. Sustainable management of resources should also be our goal. To reduce our ecological footprint, we must reduce and change our pattern of consumption. This cannot be done with more environmentally destructive employment, so working hours should be reduced and diverted into environmental work. The introduction of a 4-day week would result in a reduction in consumption of up to 20%, as long as nothing else changes. However, since more leisure time certainly leads to more consumption, we need to think about the production side of the economy. Before this happens in the following section on the Green New Deal, we now come to the third and final dimension of stabilizing economic policy: trade policy.

4.4 International Trade

Trade policy is the third major instrument of macroeconomic policy, alongside monetary and fiscal policy. The main factors influencing trade are the nominal exchange rate and the changes in nominal wages and productivity, which are reflected in the change in unit labor costs. It is fundamental that the countries are not actors that export and import themselves. Even when we talk about "American exports", we actually mean exports by American companies. Balance of payments statistics simply record transactions between residents (Americans) and non-residents (non-Americans).

The real side of international trade

Basically, trade policy and international trade can be discussed from two perspectives. On the one hand, exports are a loss of produced goods (and services, hereafter referred to as "goods") that are not available for domestic consumption. Exports therefore make a country's population tighten its belt as it consumes less than it produces. This will affect distribution. If, for example, wages grow only weakly relative to foreign countries, an ever-larger share of production will (have to) be sold to foreigners at a fixed exchange rate, as their purchasing power grows faster than at home due to relatively high wage increases. As a result, export companies to whom corporate profits are distributed will gain.

If we choose an extreme example the problem becomes very clear. With wages at zero dollars per hour, all production would be exported, and domestic consumption would be zero. This real (referring to goods and services as opposed to the monetary dimension) perspective considers only the goods side of trade. From this perspective, exports are foregone consumption and thus welfare-reducing. If we let wages rise more quickly, more and more production will be sold domestically and exports will fall. We can guess that workers and employees prefer higher wages and corporate income earners do not. Rising exports can therefore be a sign of stagnating wages. This results in higher profits for exporters and a corresponding redistribution.[22]

Relatively low wages have historically been experienced in many colonies, which often led to high exports and low imports. Adam Smith, the great-grandfather of economics, had this to say about the blessings of the division of labor in his great 1776 work "An Inquiry into the Nature and Causes of the Wealth of Nations"[23]:

> It is the great multiplication of the productions of all the different arts, in consequence of the division of labor, which occasions, in a well-governed society, that universal opulence which extends itself to the lowest ranks of the people.

Low wages would certainly not allow general prosperity to reach the lowest classes of society, as Adam Smith assumed it would in a "well-governed society". In this respect, wages are of very great importance when considering international trade. Thus, while exports represent foregone consumption for nationals, imports are additional consumption from this perspective. Imports allow consumption over and above domestic production. Imports thus represent an increase in consumption opportunities. Here, too, a thought experiment can help. A situation is conceivable in which a country produces nothing and consumption consists entirely of imports. This is a characteristic of structures consisting of core or metropolis and hinterland or colonies. In the center, money is generated and spent, allowing consumption over and above domestic production. In the periphery, the money is saved, which means that nothing is ever demanded from the metropolis. Perhaps people

---

[22] It is also the conclusion reached by the International Monetary Fund (IMF 2019) for Germany, for example.
[23] Smith (1776, 13).

there have to use the money to pay taxes, or the money is used to buy real estate in the metropolis. The flow of consumer goods then flows in only one direction, from periphery to metropolis.

The monetary side of international trade

The other perspective that must always be considered is the monetary side of the generation of expenditures and incomes. In a modern monetary economy, goods are not bartered but bought with money. We all know that in the purchase of goods, no distinction is made between domestic and foreign goods. When we buy foreign goods in a supermarket, we pay as usual with our bank card, cash, or credit card. When we buy goods abroad, we also pay in this way. Anyone who has made a purchase abroad can confirm that normal means of payment (bank card, credit card, cash, etc.) can be used. Consumption by US citizens abroad also counts toward US imports as they increase domestic consumption. We do not incur debts in the regions where we go on vacation. We merely cede assets in the form of payment instruments (cash, bank balances, promises of payment connected to credit cards).

From the perspective of income and expenditure, exports are net inflows for the exporter. Either they lead to higher foreign assets (if residents hold more claims against non-residents, e.g., in the form of Euros or Japanese government bonds), or they reduce foreign liabilities (e.g., if non-domestic residents pay with domestic currency, which then becomes the property of domestic residents). Exports thus lead to net asset inflows, imports to net asset outflows. Again, it is important to note that these are only statistics. A country is not an active agent and therefore cannot have net inflows or outflows—only residents can experience such changes in wealth.[24]

Exports and employment

This view is important because money can only be spent once by each individual. Thus, if a domestic consumer buys foreign apples, which may be cheaper, instead of domestic apples, purchasing power moves from the account of a domestic consumer to the account of the foreign exporter. This removes purchasing power from the domestic monetary circuit and can have a corresponding negative impact on employment. The foreign exporter is less likely to spend the money on domestic goods than the American apple producer would have done. It all depends on the individual case.

Since exports lead to additional net inflows and thus to additional income, they increase employment—unless there is already full employment.[25] Since

---

[24] Residents include firms and the state.
[25] At full employment, more aggregate demand will very likely lead to rising wages and prices.

full employment has not prevailed for decades, it is therefore the normal case that additional exports create more employment. Companies hire more employees and produce more if they can sell more. Exports increase the demand for goods and therefore have an expansionary effect on an economy.

Conversely, imports that replace domestic production reduce the potential demand for domestic goods. Domestic firms sell less. Imports thus lead to additional income abroad, and thus purchasing power is lost for the domestic monetary circuit. This need not be a problem if, say, the additional shift in demand to imports is offset by an expansion of demand in other categories: more consumption, more government spending, more private investment, or more exports. If this is not the case, however, then an increase in imports does not lead to an increase in employment—which is a decline in relative terms.

Export surplus or import surplus?

International trade is a double-edged sword. On the one hand, exports increase incomes and reduce consumption; on the other, imports reduce incomes and increase consumption. Which position is better for a country: export surplus or import surplus? While the US has been a net importer for the last decades, countries like China, Japan, and Germany celebrate themselves as the world's export champions. So, the answer to this question is anything but clear. The questions of distribution, the monetary system, and international debt positions play a major role. Before we put on our national glasses, let's take a look at the global economy. The world economy's unemployment rate is currently just under 5%.[26] What can explain the remaining global unemployment?

As we saw above, unemployment is the result of a lack of demand (given working hours and technology). If we divide the world into a private (households and businesses) and a public sector (governments), we recognize that the combined net spending of both sectors today is not sufficient for full employment, given the savings desires of the private sector. An increase in spending or a reduction in the savings rate in at least one of the two sectors would be necessary to create more employment. Since the government cannot force households and businesses to increase spending for the good of the global economy or even the national economy, it can be rightly argued that existing unemployment is due to government under-spending. Alternatively, we could reduce working hours with full wage compensation (so that monthly nominal wages are stable). Businesses would thus have to

---

[26] https://data.worldbank.org/indicator/SL.UEM.TOTL.ZS.

look for additional employees. Work would now be redistributed with the same volume of work (the number of hours worked). The advantage of this idea is that the consumption would not increase further or even decrease.[27] A 4-day week or even a 30-h week would be conceivable.

The logic of expenditures and revenues

It is a fundamental insight that in a 2-sector model of the world economy income and expenditure must be equal. Every expenditure leads to an income, and every income is triggered by an expenditure. It does not work the other way around. Nobody can decide simply to have a higher income, which then increases expenditures elsewhere! There is also income that does not lead to expenditures. That money is saved. The starting point is therefore always spending. The saving (= income not spent) of one sector corresponds to the deficit (gap between spending and income) of the other sector. A sector can only take in more than it spends if the other sectors spend more than they take in. Saving and increasing (net) debt are necessarily two sides of the same coin.

4.5 Sectoral Balances, Exchange Rates, and Unit Labor Costs

We can now broaden this perspective and consider a national economy instead of the world economy. For this purpose, we divide the economy into two parts, domestic and foreign. Then, we further divide the domestic sector into private sector (households and firms) and public sector (government at all levels). For these three sectors, again, net financial saving of one sector must equal the deficit of at least one of the other two sectors. The change in net financial saving of all three sectors must add up to zero, since total income and total expenditure must be identical.

We understand that the two domestic sectors can only save together if the external sector—the households, firms and governments in foreign countries in the rest of the world—goes into debt or reduces its net assets (which corresponds to a deficit). This is the case when a country has a surplus in its trade balance (exports > imports). Not all countries can be net savers at the same time, because one country's trade surplus is equal to another country's trade deficit. The balances are straightforward when the government aims for

---

[27] This depends, among other things, on whether nominal wages will be stable though working hours are reduced or not.

and actually achieves a balanced budget. When tax revenues equal government spending, then the private sector as a whole can only save (earn income surpluses) by selling more goods abroad than vice versa. However, private savings come at the cost of rising net debt (or a decline in net wealth) abroad. In the medium term, there is a threat of a collapse in foreign demand and perhaps a financial crisis abroad.

The implications of a balanced trade account are also interesting. When it is balanced, surpluses must inevitably have been incurred by households and companies at the expense of a government deficit. There is no other way: when the private sector has earned more than it spends, then tax revenues must have been below the level of government spending. Since we know that private debt is risky and public debt usually is not (the federal government cannot run out of money and can always "pay its debts"), this constellation seems to make sense from a financial stability point of view.

Figure 4.3 shows the US sectoral balances. The sum of the sectoral balances of the private sector (black), the public sector (gray), and the foreign sector (light gray) is always zero. It can be seen that the private sector has been running a much higher surplus after the financial crash of 2008/09. This was to repair the damage done by the financial crash. The same pattern is visible before the "New Economy" crashed. In expectation of ever-rising share prices, households and firms let their debt increase in the late 1990s so the sector as a whole was in deficit. This change in private behavior, caused by saving less and investing more (in capital goods and real estate), caused the public surpluses of the Clinton administration via the increase in tax revenues that came with the economic boom. When it finally collapsed, the fiscal surplus turned to deficit again.

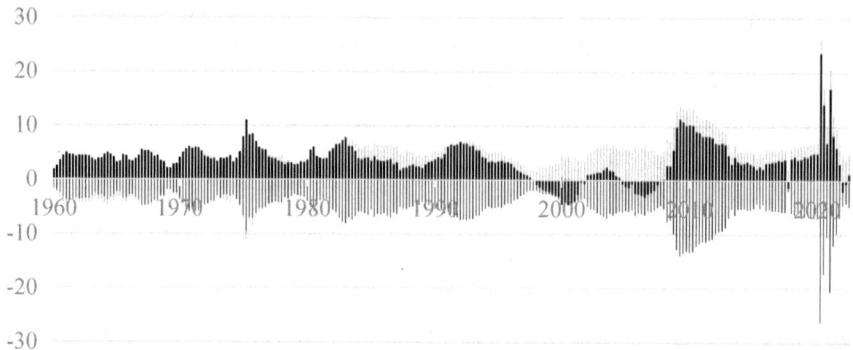

Fig. 4.3 Balances for the private (black), public (gray), and external sectors (light gray), in percent of GDP. *Source* BEA (W994RC, A191RC, AD01RC) and Board of Governors of the Federal Reserve System (FA265000905)

4 Modern Money Theory as Part of Economics

After 2008–09, American firms and households were repairing their balance sheets. They saved more to pay down debt and to replace assets lost or written down. Around 2014, this process ended and the economy grew without much inflation, which only increased toward the end of the decade. The pandemic hit the US economy in spring 2020, causing the expected 1-trillion-dollar public deficit of that year to turn into a 3-trillion-dollar public deficit. Since the government's red ink is our black ink, as Stephanie Kelton always stresses, there was nothing wrong with that. That income was needed to get the economy going again after the worst of the pandemic was behind us. There was absolutely no problem of finding the money, and those who said that financing a public deficit is always ensured were proven to be correct.

Private debt

Within the private sector, we can separate companies and households. Households wish to be net savers, as they save for old age. In the process, parts of income are withheld via social security contributions, so that most of us would not be able to spend our entire income. Those who spend more than they earn will have financed this through a loan or running down assets. But since the loans have to be repaid, financial risk increases. Households may lose their income due to unemployment and thus have trouble with repayment. If, for example, households buy a house with a real estate loan, they can "survive" with negative equity as long as they can afford the repayments. Working in a job with a monthly income stabilizes this financial arrangement.

The situation is different for companies. They must always be solvent. However, some operate with external debt and might be able to keep their expenditure level above their income level for decades (while selling shares or bonds). The important thing here is that further financing is ensured via the financial market. However, the revenue surpluses of companies or the corporate sector are something different from profits. The latter generally are the result of accounting and not directly related to the cash flow. In the US, companies ran deficits for decades and it is only since the 2000s that the sector has shown relatively constant surpluses. Parallel saving by households, companies, and the state would only possible if other countries play along and take on the role of the big debtor. That is unlikely to happen as the US experienced persistent trade account deficits in recent decades.

Flexible exchange rates and inflation

In industrialized countries, changes in nominal exchange rates lead to little or no change in the prices of export and import goods. Thus, even a devaluation of one's own currency does not normally lead to an increased rate of inflation.

For example, the Icelandic krona depreciated by more than 50% against the dollar during the Icelandic financial crisis in the mid-2000s. However, the inflation rate rose "only" briefly to just under 20% and then settled between 2 and 5%. Unemployment quickly fell back towards 2 to 3%, and a depression like the one in Greece some years later was avoided. Iceland is a small and open economy; for somewhat larger countries, the results are even less pronounced. For example, the exchange rate between the Canadian dollar and the US dollar is flexible, sometimes fluctuating by 50%. Nevertheless, the inflation rates of both countries correlate and do not diverge when the exchange rate changes, as Fig. 4.4 shows.

Fig. 4.4 US and Canadian dollar exchange rates (black line, right axis) and inflation rates in the USA (black dotted line) and Canada (gray dotted line). *Source* FRED.stlouisfed.org (BLS, Board of Governors, World Bank)

5

What is Economic Policy?

Active economic policy should not be taken for granted. Until the beginning of the twentieth century, most economists believed that the economy was self-regulating. Economic policy would be unnecessary or even prevented automatic adjustment processes within the capitalist system. The idea was that all expenditures of firms on wages and other factors of production (inputs, raw materials, energy, rent, etc.) would automatically become income for the owners of these factors, which would then spend all their income. Costs of production would always create the money that would later purchase this production. Therefore, every supply of goods and services would be demanded in the economy. The economic cycle would be stable. The demand for goods and services (i.e., what people buy with their money) would be as high as the supply of goods and services at all times. Purchasing power could be retired by saving when households take their money to the bank. However, banks would lend this money to businesses, which would use it to finance their investments. So, even saving would not take purchasing power away.

The economy was assumed to be always at full employment as long as firms paid wages based on productivity. Any unemployment would either be voluntary—workers would not want to work at the existing wage—or caused by wages being at a high level which discouraged firms from hiring. Unions and workers would be to blame for too high wages.

5.1 Theory and Practice

Unfortunately, these ideas are wrong, even if they seem somewhat logically consistent. Involuntary unemployment, as we saw in the pandemic, is a very big problem. In the aftermath of the euro crisis in 2010–14, it was also obvious that unemployment rates of over 20% are within the realm of possibility and that the economies of Spain or Greece, for example, did not recover as the theory of a stable economy would have it. It was certainly not due to excessive wage demands. In addition, the monetary theory is incorrect: banks do not and cannot lend out the savings of depositors! We will consider a more accurate description of the process below.

In the aftermath of the pandemic, the federal government reacted by increasing government spending. The Fed brought the interest rate back to zero. Checks for $2,500 were sent out to citizens to get the economy going again when the lockdowns were lifted and the pandemic retreated. Different acts were legislated that increased expenditures at the federal level by hundreds of billions of dollars. This idea goes back to the Great Depression, which began with the Great (stock market) Crash of 1929. Mass unemployment and the economic decline of large communities in the USA and around the world were the result of a precipitous drop in private investment. In Germany, Adolf Hitler came to power as a result of the austerity policies of the German government, which were unsuitable for dealing with the crisis. In the US, President Franklin D. Roosevelt introduced a new economic policy program with the New Deal in 1933 after four years of economic stagnation, mass unemployment, and poverty. It was obvious to all observers that the economy would not rebound without help. Government spending was increased significantly and permanently (with the exception of 1937) to combat the crisis, returning to a normal rate of unemployment even before the US entry in World War II. Direct job creation by the government played the most important role, though most economists "remember" public works programs like the Golden Gate bridge (Attewell 2018).[1]

After World War II, it was realized that people cannot live together peacefully if mass unemployment and inequality of wealth and income dissolve social cohesion. Individuals always grow up in the society they form at the same time. If social justice is no longer present people become existentially anxious, turning against social structures and often becoming aggressive. Therefore, a society must ensure that distribution and employment are

---

[1] Probably Keynes (1936) had something to do with the way we "remember" the Great Depression, arguing in the last chapter of his *General Theory* that "a somewhat comprehensive socialisation of investment will prove the only means of securing an approximation to full employment".

designed for the benefit of all. The market, as the British economist John Maynard Keynes recognized, is not capable of creating this situation. The economy, he realized, is not a self-regulating system (Keynes 1963 [1935]). The state must therefore strive for an economic policy that provides a sufficient number of jobs and generates incomes and wealth that correspond to the population's sense of justice.

The economy and money

The main driving force of the economy is the demand for (meaning spending on) goods and services. When demand increases, companies increase their production, expand their capacities (generating new capital in the form of machines, buildings, etc.), and hire new employees. Thus, the level of spending determines not only production, but also the level of employment. Involuntary unemployment is the result of too little spending on goods and services and too much net saving. It can be eliminated through higher spending.[2] But where does this additional spending come from? In our modern monetary system, we distinguish between the creator of money and the users of money.

In the British colony of Virginia, as we saw in Chap. 3, a so-called paper money existed before the Declaration of Independence. The government forced citizens to pay taxes in its own currency, which were called "notes". The state printed notes and spent them. Through taxes, the notes were returned to the government and—burned! Since the state could print new notes at low cost, it was cheaper to print new money instead of reusing old money. The colonial government of Virginia was thus able to "pay for" its expenses and did not need any income to "finance" the expenditures beforehand. Businesses and households, on the other hand, were users of money. They finance any additional spending either by drawing down assets, borrowing, or issuing share certificates or fixed-rate securities (bonds).

5.2 The Circular Flow of Income

From a macroeconomic perspective, the objective of economic activity is the production of (public and private) goods and services and their distribution. Figure 5.1 explains the money and income circuit. In a monetary economy, citizens do not consume what they produce. This would not be desirable

---

[2] Changing net saving is the other option, but that is difficult to do and takes time. The federal government could increase pension payments, for instance, so that citizens will spend more of today's incomes and save less.

due to the division of labor. It is better we receive money for our work in the form of income. (Those who cannot work should receive a just income from the state.) With this, we can buy what we want. At the center of the circuit lies consumption, around which everything ultimately revolves. For households, money is only a means to an end, namely the satisfaction of needs (consumption) that have not been addressed by public goods and services (like public health care or public roads). For companies, too, money is only a means to an end, namely the generation of profits. Last but not least, the state uses money as a means to an end, to provision itself with the resources it needs to serve the public purpose.

Expenditures are met by spending money. As shown in Fig. 5.1, there are three main sources and outflows of money. These are (source followed by outflow):

- Government spending and taxes.
- Private investment and saving (defined as unspent income).
- Exports and imports.

Additional income can be created by the federal government when it spends more money into existence. Companies and households can also increase their spending. To do this, they take out a loan from a bank, sell bonds or assets. They spend the money, creating additional income. Last, foreign countries can also affect the domestic economy. Exports that foreigners pay for (in whatever currency) increase the income of domestic residents.

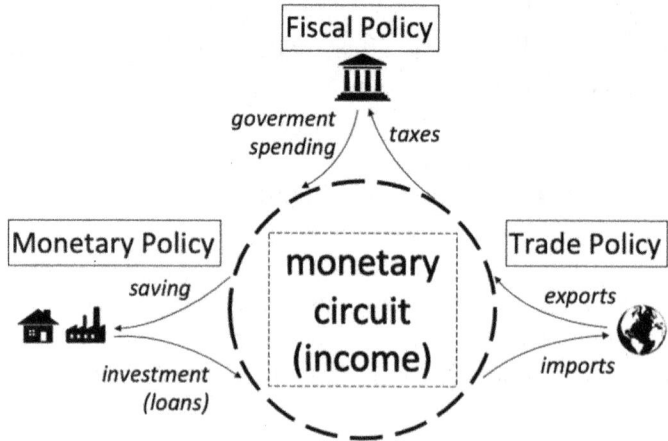

Fig. 5.1 Economic policy and the income cycle. *Source* Own figure, with help from Nathalie Freitag

Money can also flow out of the circulation. This happens, among other things, when households or companies save. In doing so, they set money aside—that part of their incomes has not been spent. The goal of saving might be to build up assets or to reduce debt. In the latter case, the bank deposits disappear forever. This is also the case when the state collects taxes. Bank deposits and reserves are permanently removed from circulation. A temporary gap arises when imports are paid for. The money ends up in the accounts of foreigners. Whether and when they will spend their income on domestic goods is uncertain.

The monetary cycle will turn quickly if a lot of spending takes place. Companies invest a lot, the government spends a lot (at all levels), and the rest of the world wants to buy more and more of our export goods—if one or two of these circumstances are met, companies will probably ramp up their production. They can sell everything they produced. If they purchase more raw materials and more labor, some prices or wages might go up. Companies can easily pass on these cost increases to consumers by raising the prices of their goods and services. If this happens at the same time in many companies, the inflation rate may also rise.

Alternatively, economically weak times with little spending in the three sectors may be expected to be accompanied by stable and/or low rates of inflation. Since some companies cannot sell their entire product range, they might reduce prices. After all, they need money to pay back their debts. The cycle is weakening. If there are not enough jobs available, some job seekers will inevitably be left without work. Since it is not possible to save labor—someone who does not work one year cannot work twice as much in the second year—it would probably make sense to create more jobs.

Economic policy instruments

In economically weak times, this does not happen automatically. Only higher spending would induce companies to expand their production again. A modern sovereign state has three instruments at its disposal for this purpose (higher spending to create more employment):

- Monetary policy (key interest rate).
- Fiscal policy (government spending, tax rates).
- Trade policy (exchange rate, wages if necessary).

These three instruments are designed to enable the state to respond to so-called fluctuations in the business cycle. They are also intended to help achieve goals such as full employment, price stability, and sustainable economic activity. There is now a very big debate among economists about how these instruments actually work and what their effects are. There are major disagreements, for instance, about the role of monetary policy. Recent experience seems to indicate that higher interest rates are not causing an economy to fall into a recession nor do they reduce the rate of inflation. Instead, higher government spending seems to induce higher private investment as private firms jockey for public sector orders. As long as there are workers available so that these can be hired at current wages, there is no reason to believe that this will have an effect on wage growth and the rate of inflation. Energy prices have been falling in 2023 and are now more or less constant, which means that there is no cost-push to be expected from this either. Larry Summers argued in summer 2022 that in order to bring the rate of inflation down it would be necessary to increase the rate of unemployment. The following 18 months have shown this view to be wrong. Employment went up and inflation down. The idea that we would have to throw millions of workers into unemployment so that the rest can enjoy price stability is not only morally repulsive, it is also unnecessary. Why would economists ask millions of workers to suffer unemployment when stable prices can be had at full employment?

Setting the interest rate

So, if the interest rate is not the central lever in the economy, then what should the central bank do with its interest rates? Should the Federal Reserve Bank just stop changing it? There seems to be a case for stable interest rates as these surely would help businesses with their planning. They would know the costs of borrowing money more or less in advance—it is simply the interbank market interest rate set by the Fed plus some risk factor that depends on the firm's financial health. Eliminating volatile interest rates would help firms especially with long-term plans because interest rates in the future matter most for projects that stretch over decades. Less uncertainty would help somewhat with long-term investment, but nevertheless would not remove all the uncertainty that firms and households face.

"Parking" the interest rate is therefore a popular idea in economic policy circles (Watts 2021). Warren Mosler suggested that the "natural" interest rate is zero (Forstater and Mosler 2005). If central banks did not intervene, the interest rate on the interbank market would drop to zero. So why not leave it there? After all, any positive interest rate translates into unearned income for bond holders, who usually are relatively rich. A zero interest rate would redistribute wealth from rich to poor. Another idea would be to set the interest rate at the inflation target level. That way, monetary wealth can be carried into the future by holding government bonds. Over the decades, these would return the purchasing power that was given up in the past—if the inflation target had been hit. It would allow self-employed workers and firms to save in order to spend in the future outside of the public pension system (which can never run out of money so that solvency is never an issue, independent from the nominal pension payments the federal government makes in the future).

How much should the federal government spend?

Given the inability of monetary policy to steer the real economy, fiscal policy takes on a more pronounced role. Its effect is more direct since every dollar the government spends translates into a dollar of income or revenue for US firms and households, often increasing output directly as the government orders goods and services that are built on demand (and not commodities which would be supplied by firms anyway). In the following pages, three possible scenarios for fiscal policy guidance will be presented, starting with today's MMT-informed approach, followed by the "new" Keynesian and then the "old" Keynesian approach.

From our new perspective, the state is the monopoly supplier of currency. Having imposed tax liabilities in the state's currency, the state has turned households and firms into sellers of labor, goods and services, and other resources. It has also created involuntary unemployment, since not all workers might find a job. Since only the state can create currency at zero cost and it created the involuntary unemployment in the first place, it is only logical that it should address the unemployment problem. The question is only how it will spend enough money to create full employment and price stability. How it pays is not a relevant question—as always through the Fed, which acts as the fiscal agent of the state.

The solution preferred by most MMT economists is a combination of net expenditure by the government geared toward full employment plus the Job Guarantee. This two-step should erase all involuntary unemployment in the economy. It would be important also because poverty is connected to unemployment, and creating jobs for the unemployed is the same as fighting poverty. It is not the fault of the unemployed that they cannot find a job—there are just not enough jobs around (workers shortages in some sectors are no indication of full employment). At least since the 1970s, mass unemployment has been a "normal" condition of the USA and other Western economies. That was unnecessary. There is no "economic law" that says that some workers need to be unemployed. History shows us that unemployment rates of 2–4% were reality in the US before the 1970s. Other countries' experiences show us that even less unemployment is possible. There is no need to sacrifice price stability as these low rates of unemployment were reached together with low rates of inflation.

Acting on information

So, government net expenditure should be geared toward full employment. This means that we need to have some information about the state of the economy. First of all, we would need to know how many labor hours are still available. This measure includes labor hours that would be provided by those that are currently involuntarily unemployed, but also from those that would prefer to work more or in jobs with higher qualifications (underemployment). The measure could also include labor hours that could be brought to bear from those that are voluntarily unemployed but would return to work if labor market conditions were better. One way to increase participation in the labor force would be to increase the quantity and quality of public goods and services, like better health care and longer maternity leave.

The federal government should also have a rough idea of where un(der)employed workers are and what their skills and knowledge look like. It is important to target spending in a way that brings resources into the economy without adversely affecting price stability. Put differently, the government should create jobs that are tailored to the available workers and their location—instead of trying to hire workers in professions where unemployment is close to non-existent in locations where unemployment is close to non-existent.

The government should have projects ready for a wide variety of locations and workers. It can be assumed that local governments would know best about what communities need. In order to avoid giving more power to the federal government, the general rule should be that decisions about spending should be as close to the citizens as possible. Spending at the state and municipal level is much better suited to target unemployment than spending at the federal level, where it is not clear at what locations the spending will finally occur. For instance, it makes little sense for the federal government to create a public bank in New York City (it would hire bankers) and a technology center in Silicon (hiring IT workers). This would only result in making these local bottlenecks worse, driving up wages in the respective sectors and also real estate prices. It would probably increase the incomes of the rich and leave the poor unaffected.

Fiscal policy and job guarantee together

The federal government hence adjusts its spending—given current taxes and tax rates—as to bring about full employment. Since economic planning is never perfect, it can be expected that net spending by the government still falls short. For those who still cannot find work, the Job Guarantee, discussed in detail in the next chapter, would provide an anchor. It offers work for those who can and want to work. Put simply, it turns the un(der)employed into full-time workers—if they want to work (full-time)—and helps to erase poverty and improve the skills and knowledge of the work force.

While there is mass unemployment, there is no conflict between the public and the private sector. Private firms can hire workers just as the public sector can. Once there are labor shortages, the game changes. The government, being the monopoly issuer of currency, could offer any wage necessary to draw workers to its side. The private firms are restricted in the wages that they can offer, since they are money users. They have to make sure that they can pay all their debts and they also know that their debt cannot grow too quickly. So, when does the government stop spending?

Opportunity costs

Since the federal government "pays for" its spending by money creation of the Federal Reserve Bank, there are no direct "costs" in terms of dollars. Whereas we have to think very hard about our spending, because we can only spend every dollar once, the federal government is not bound by a budget constraint. However, spending is not "free" in the sense that resources that are used by the government cannot be used by anyone else. This is why the government should think hard about whether it wants to spend on any project. After all, the resources that are used up are not available for other uses. A different way to express this is that the government should look at opportunity costs.

Opportunity costs is a very old economic concept. The main point is the understanding that economic resources can be used in different ways leading to different outcomes. If resources are used to produce a public service X, they cannot be used to provide a private good Y. The loss of the consumption of private good Y is the opportunity cost of the production of public service X. Here is an example. Let's say the federal government hires engineers to redesign cities in order to cope with climate change. It is possible that the government can just hire these engineers at the going wage because there are many unemployed engineers. In that case, the opportunity costs are zero because the engineers would not be producing anything.

If, however, all engineers are already working, then significant opportunity costs exist. For sure, they produce goods and services that are valued by the nation because otherwise it would not be profitable to employ them. (While this is very likely for engineers, other professions might be profitable, but their impact on society might be negative because of value extraction.) So, if these engineers switched to the public sector, they would not produce these private goods and services anymore. The value of these goods and services is the opportunity costs of these engineers. If the goods and services they produce in the public sector are worth more to society than the opportunity costs, it would still be a good idea to move the workers. However, the valuation of public goods and services is difficult. Often, no market exists, and hence there is no price that can be used as the basis of valuation. Instead, the valuation is directly based on the costs, which means on the wages of the engineers. Therefore, while theoretically the concept of opportunity costs is clear-cut, the reality is more complicated. The public value created by those engineers might be significantly higher than the wages they are paid.

The federal government might chose to ignore the whole approach and spend money as it sees fit. This would be a big problem if the federal government never changed. However, in elections citizens vote for their representatives, which will determine future government spending. If a government neglects opportunity costs and talks up public goods and services, but voters don't see it that way, they will vote for the opposition party and through this change the scope of government spending. This is what politics should really be about when it comes to fiscal policy. It is not about how to *pay for* things or how to *finance* government spending—it is about the use of resources for the public purpose and the corresponding opportunity costs.

What can we afford?

The federal government can afford anything that it can buy from the non-government sector (which includes firms, households, and the rest of the world) and anything that it can build itself or provide in the public sector. Can we afford to put a man on the moon? Yes. Can we afford a public pension system? Yes. Can we afford Medicare and Medicaid, now and forever? Yes. Can we afford to eradicate poverty? Yes. Can we, through the Job Guarantee, afford to give a job to everyone who can and wants to work? Yes. Can we afford to green our economy? Yes. Can we afford to produce over and beyond the resources that we have? No.

Of course, politics is not about physical limits of resources. It is about what we want to do with our resources. What kind of society do we want? Which resources are we willing to sacrifice to reach certain policy goals? What should be the role of the government? What should be individual responsibility? Are there human and economic rights that the state has to guarantee, like the right to property or the right to work? What public infrastructure does the private sector need to be dynamic and innovative, and what do citizens need to be free from fear and happy? How can private and public sector best work together? How can we minimize corruption? How can we ensure that power is balanced and neither centralized nor in the hands of a few families?

All these are not genuinely economic questions. They are political questions that can be analyzed economically using the lens of Modern Monetary Theory. MMT can help to understand the trade-offs that are necessarily involved with some issues and not with others. It can help to examine possible solutions for a variety of problems. MMT does not "fix" anything. It is a lens that can provide us with one very insightful perspective, but it should not be seen as the only lens. Some people might think that MMT is not a useful lens and that is ok (freedom of speech, right?). For some problems, MMT probably is not a useful lens. It is not a theory of everything. MMT could be connected with other lenses to analyze policy problems from all areas of economic and social policy. One area of economic policy where MMT can make a contribution is the modern business cycle.

5.3 The Modern Business Cycle

The business cycle consists of different phases. It is usually measured in terms of the change in GDP and employment, which usually move in the same direction. Two quarters of negative rates of economic growth are considered to count as a recession. A recession is also called a slump. It does not necessarily degenerate into a depression (like in the 1930s) or a financial crisis (like in 2008–09). Recessions usually last some quarters and are fought by economic policy. Usually, the central bank decreases its interest rates and the federal government increases net spending. The resulting improvement leads to an upward phase. Once the economy runs hot, we speak of a boom. The boom at some point turns into a bust, another recession results. The business cycle is complete.

One very important question is what causes the economy to behave like this. There have been different theories developed over the decades and centuries. The ups and downs of the economy have been blamed on sunspots, agricultural periods of plenty, credit creation by commercial banks, and much more. While some of these theories might be compatible with each other, we focus on monetary theories of production. In a world where money matters, firms produce when consumers spend money. This explains the boom and bust. How does spending translate into changes in production and employment?

Spending, production, and employment

When consumers spend less on goods and services, sales will drop. Stockpiles grow until the firm decides to cut production. That is ultimately necessary because firms borrow money to finance production and have to service and repay their debts. Firms need to earn income. Increasing stockpiles is not bad, but debts have to be paid in money and not in kind. So, less demand for goods and services from consumers translates into lower production. If firms produce less, they need less workers. They are hence likely to lay off workers, maybe only temporarily at first, then permanently. They might also not hire new workers when old workers retire or let workers move to other firms.

When consumers spend more money on goods and services, firms will see their sales increase. They will be happy to increase output to increase profits and gain market share. Producing more output will mean hiring more workers. Output and employment generally move in the same direction. To produce more, a firm might hire only a few extra workers in the beginning. Once it hits capacity, it might decide to expand by upgrading old equipment or buying new equipment. Perhaps a new plant is built at some point. All of this increases demand for workers and hence employment.

Since this happens in time, it is a dynamic process. It is likely that there are second round and third round effects as workers that are hired spend more money on consumption goods. The increase in demand feeds back into the initial increase in demand. Firms are more optimistic, expecting output to increase in the future. They might be tempted to increase their investment earlier and invest more if they expect consumer spending to rise significantly in the future.

From boom …

A crucial question is how it is possible that demand for goods and services in the economy can increase. How can spending go up? The answer is that some units in the economy must have decided to spend more money. This is about spending, not about "money". The economic units that form the economy are households, firms, the government, and the rest of the world. Theoretically, any class of economic units can cause a boom. It does not matter much for businesses whether they sell more to households, other firms, the government or economic units in the rest of the word—they will react by expanding output.

It is therefore an empirical question what is driving a boom. Theoretically, all economic units can increase their spending. Firms and households can decide to spend more of their income or sell assets to finance additional spending or go into debt by borrowing money from banks or selling bonds. Since firms are users of money they will be only willing to do that if they believe that the money they invest will eventually come back to them, plus a dividend or interest rate or appreciation of the share price. This is what Hyman Minsky called the capitalist process: giving up money today in expectation of more money tomorrow.

The federal government is the issuer of currency. It is not constrained by these kind of considerations. It can just spend more money if it has the political will. This is why the federal government is the natural candidate to lead the economy from bust to boom. It can always spend more if there are firms willing to sell goods or services to the government for money. So, there is no economic depression that cannot be turned into a boom through the federal government's fiscal capacity. (This is Mosler's law, named after Warren Mosler.)

The *Inflation Reduction Act* of 2022 was an example of how this works. After the pandemic, the unemployment rate approached 20%. The federal government sent checks to citizens to get the economy going, and in 2022 a major spending package was announced. About $433 billion were to be invested in energy security and climate change as well as the *Affordable Care Act* extension. As a result of this additional spending, private investment has spiked as firms struggle to ramp up their production to be able to sell to the federal government.

… to bust.

So, it is the federal government which can increase spending to put the economy on an upward trajectory. Why then does the boom stop and turn into a bust? The answer to this question can be explained through an analysis of the board game Monopoly. Players are competing to buy real estate, charging rent to other players, and using their income to buy more real estate, which means they will charge even more rent to other players until eventually the game results in a monopoly. That is what the inventor of the game wanted to show, so that people would understand the winner-takes-it-all logic of the real estate sector. Somehow, though, our human drive to always be number one turned the game into a huge success while the original intention has fallen into the background.

Anyway, an interesting feature of the game is "the bank". One player has to play the bank, which makes payments and collects money from players on different occasions. Random events take place in the game which sometimes lead to players getting more money from the bank and sometimes paying money to the bank. Another very interesting idea is the field named "GO". Players crossing that field get some extra money from the bank every single turn. This is very much like a government that spends more dollars into the economy than it collects via tax revenues. This is also the reason why the Monopoly game never ends in the bankruptcy of all players—there is always a winner. Why? Let's see what happens when we turn the "GO" field around.

If all players passing the "GO" field had to pay some money to the bank (taxes), the game would probably not lead to "irrational exuberance" (Alan Greenspan). Players would quickly understand their budget constraint and act more prudently. Since they will have to pay rent and taxes it is a clever strategy not to spend too much money. After all, taxes and rents are payable in money. Illiquid real estate in the form of streets, houses, and hotels is second-best. The Monopoly game would end with the same result—a monopoly—but the road there would be a deflationary road in which money is drained out of the monetary circulation.

From public deficit to surplus

Let's move from Monopoly back to the US economy. Figure 5.2 shows the net injections of the government into the US economy, which is the equivalent of the bank in Monopoly. When the bank/government net injects lots of dollars, the line is deeply negative, like during the pandemic. The US government spent more than it took back in the form of tax revenues in 2020, with the difference making up more than 14% of GDP. This was because of falling tax revenues in the wake of a slumping economy and rising government spending. But what about the bust?

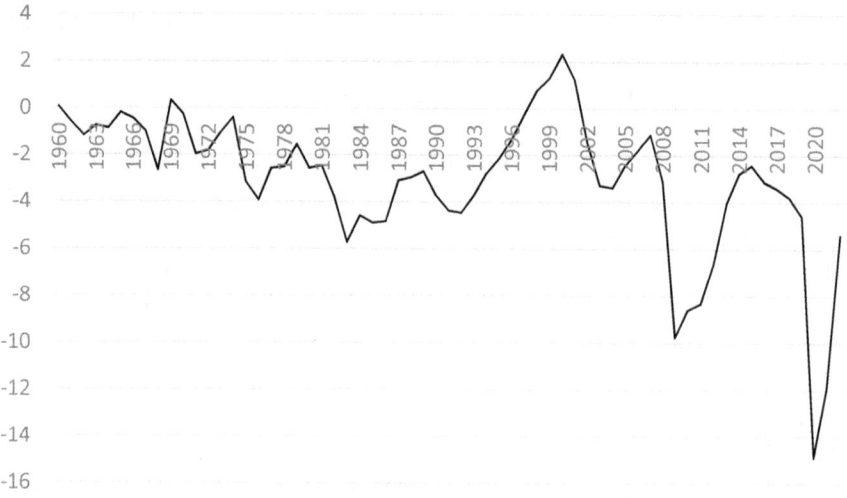

Fig. 5.2 Fiscal surplus or deficit, 1960–2022, in percent of GDP. *Source* FRED, https://fred.stlouisfed.org/series/FYFSGDA188S

The recessions of 2001–2002 and 2008–2009 were both preceded by a shrinking public deficit that even turned into a public surplus in the late 1990s. The government injected less and less money just before the recessions. This very likely translated into diminished expectations of sales for private sector firms. When the government takes more money out of circulation via tax revenues then it injects via government spending, firms and households have less money. It is only natural to expect them to spend less as well. This would translate into less sales, and firms would eventually cut output, which then leads to a fall in GDP and a reduction in employment.

This effect is probably magnified by the expectation that the central bank will cut interest rates in a possible recession, which would cut off hundreds of billions of interest income for the holders of government bonds. The way our economic system operates, the government must pro-actively increase spending in order to get the economy going again after a recession or depression. The bust comes automatically because during the boom the tax revenues increase, taking more and more money out of circulation. Government spending does not increase when tax revenues increase, so the financial situation of the private sector decreases until households and firms cut spending. A recession results.

Public and private spending

In the 1920s, the business cycle was called the trade cycle and the public sector was still very small. Trade cycles were driven by private investment as the federal government spent very little money measured as a share in GDP. With the modern welfare states introduced in the post-World War II era, this has changed significantly. Private investment now follows public spending, as private firms are eager to sell their goods and services to the government (think military-industrial complex). The government's injection of net spending is very important, and it contributes massively to the demand for goods and services. A rise in tax revenues during the boom takes away purchasing power through higher tax revenues. That is a consequential development and probably has been the main driver of recessions for some decades already.

To some extent, this fiscal mechanism of rising tax revenues during the good times—the boom—is a good thing. It ensures that the economy does not heat up too quickly and too much. Before that happens, tax revenues increase and a part of the purchasing power of the private sector is drained. This is because tax revenues increase with income as more households cross the income thresholds into higher income tax brackets. The mechanism is called an automatic stabilizer (more on automatic stabilizers in the next chapter). It works in the boom as well as in the bust, when falling nominal incomes lead to lower tax revenues. However, there is no autopilot that stops the automatic stabilizer from moving the booming economy into a bust. Future policymakers should examine the net injection of the government and its effect on the economy in terms of resources if they want to tame the business cycle.

5.4 Banking and Banking Regulation

Commercial banks are usually seen as intermediaries, taking in bank deposits, which constitute our savings, and lending them out to the firms. They supposedly convert saving(s) into investment, which would be an important function in the economy. However, this idea of banks as intermediaries does not describe reality. Investment by the business sector is not financed by savings, but by loans and bond sales and other debt instruments, as we have already described. Banks are acting as agents of the state because they rely on cash delivery from and the payment system operated by the Federal Reserve System. Their main task is credit analysis. They should ensure that purchasing power is created for those who can pay it back later. The loans to households and firms should further the public purpose. In other words, they should somehow address the needs of society.

Banks and value creation

It makes sense from the perspective of the economy that banks lend to firms looking to expand their business. If they want to upgrade production buying more machines or hiring more workers, or building another factory or buying a competing firm in order to grow and become more efficient, then there is a public purpose behind the loan. We will benefit from more efficient production or a larger supply of consumer goods, which are in high demand (as long as the resources used in the process are managed sustainably). There will be more jobs, more goods and services, and probably lower prices as well. This translates into more employment, more consumption, and price stability. What's not to like?

Another reason for banks to extend loans is to help out families. Families with young children often do not have the money to buy a house. However, they might have incomes that would be high enough to make monthly payments to service a real estate loan. These families don't want to save money and then buy a house when the kids are teens, but they want a house when the kids are young. The bank would lend the money upfront to buy the house

5 What is Economic Policy?

with a garden, and the family would pay back their debt over the decades. It would also leave the parents with a real asset that they can sell when they are old and do not work anymore. They can sell the house and live off the money they get for it, supporting their pension income.

Banks and value extraction

However, banks can also engage in lending that does not serve the public purpose. They can lend in foreign currency to borrowers who are not aware of exchange rate risk. This could create an asset boom with devastating consequences for the borrowers. Predatory lending of this kind should not be allowed. Also, banks should not let customers bet against other customers' ability of repaying their respective loans. While this creates profits for some, it leads to losses for others. Redistributing money is not the purpose of the banking system. Banks should also be prohibited from taking on highly leveraged positions. Small changes in the valuation of assets, like real estate or shares, could wipe out large banks that are highly leveraged, like Lehman Brothers. Also, banks should not be allowed to make large bonus payments during a boom. The money will not be needed in the bust when banks suffer from a worsening of their respective balance sheet.

Banks should also be regulated in a way that the conflict of interest is minimized. If banks are at the same time dealing in shares for profit and selling shares to banks, it is logical that banks will buy shares themselves before executing customers' large orders of those very shares. Banks should not overcharge customers when it comes to paying interest on checking and credit card balances. This hurts the financially vulnerable and drives them toward bankruptcy. Banks should not give loans to foreigners as it is not in the interest of the public to spur capital development in foreign countries by creating currency which might not be repaid.

The global financial crisis[3]

The financial system is inherently unstable. Building on the work of Hyman Minsky, it is recognized that cycles of financial stability in the postwar period led to laxer standards in credit analysis, which then lead to more financial instability in the 1990s and the 2000s. The last breakdown of the financial system occurred during the Global Financial Crisis in 2008/09. It was the first since the Great Crash in 1929. What happened in the run-up to the financial crisis?

---

[3] The following pages are economic history informed by MMT. For further reading my MMT authors on the GFC see Wray (2012).

The story begins in the 1990s, when the dot-com economy—a.k.a. the *New Economy*—took shape. The *Zeitgeist* of that decade was pro-market, as the collapse of the Soviet Union was interpreted to prove that markets are more efficient than governments. It was thought that deregulation, liberalization, and the handing over of power to companies, who would then regulate themselves, would bring about the best of our societies. Historians wrote about the end of history as capitalism would be the only game in town in the twenty-first century. This view became the new normal, but there were weaknesses in that interpretation from the very beginning. First of all, there isn't *one* capitalism. American capitalism is very different from, say, French and German capitalism or Nordic capitalism as in Sweden, Norway, Denmark, and Finland. Just like there are 57 varieties of tomatoes in a certain brand of ketchup, Hyman Minsky quipped, there would be 57 varieties of capitalism.

The end of history? Not so quick!

The economic history of the world is littered with state-led episodes of rapid industrial development. One example was Japan, which by 1990 was so successful that some books claimed that Japan would lead the world as number the number one economy into the twenty-first century. Also, China industrialized in the 1990s with a program of state-led development, focused on bringing in foreign technology and exporting to the rest of the world. In this climate, the rise of the internet turned investors from risk-averse hoarders of savings into casino capitalists, starting a borrowing binge that ended with both households and firms piling up debts year after year.[4] People believed that the internet would transform business for good and were willing to pay lots of dollars to gobble up shares in dubious business ventures like Pets.com, which went bust spectacularly in November 2000.

In the wake of the dot-com bust, spending in the economy was lower than before. Demand for goods and services evaporated as laid-off workers cut their spending and firms cut their business investment. In order to revive the economy, spending needed to rise. Economic policymakers had two instruments at their disposal: fiscal and monetary policy. The Bush administration opted for monetary policy to increase aggregate demand. Lower interest rates were supposed to stimulate the economy. Private investment would pick up and then more workers would be needed to supply goods and services that would go into investment. So, what happened?

Nothing much, at first. George W. Bush was dealing with a *jobless recovery*. Then, low interest rates drove real estate further prices up. The logic behind

---

[4] This is what caused the public surpluses during the years of the Clinton administration.

this effect is quite simple. Most businesses and households, when buying real estate, estimate what they can afford to borrow based on the part of future earnings that they can spend on repaying the loan. For instance, a household may expect to be able to save $250,000 over 25 years. It would be prudent to take out a loan that can be repaid with interest in the following quarter of a century. The money available for the actual purchase of real estate depends on the rate of interest. The more interest the borrower pays to the bank, the less is available to meet the asking price of real estate.

The real estate boom

At an interest rate of zero, $250,000 could be spent on the real estate purchase since no money would go toward the payment of interest. A positive interest rate the available money to spend on real estate would be reduced. Any increase in the rate of interest will lead to higher monthly payments, reducing the amount of principal that can be borrowed. Borrowers face some uncertainty since a fixed interest rate can be agreed upon, but after 10 or 20 years to loan might have to be refinanced at a future interest rate, which is unknown today. This is why lower interest rates usually translate into higher real estate prices. Exceptions are the rule, since markets exhibit herd behavior and there are also effects from higher income. In a growing economy with lots of demand for goods and services, firms and households may be able to afford to pay higher prices for real estate because of expectations of higher incomes and hence more saving.

As economist Paul Krugman noted, Americans in the 2000s got richer by selling each other houses at rising prices. Also, banks started to engage in predatory lending. This was driven by the low interest rates that the Federal Reserve Bank set for the economy. At low interest rates, life insurances, pension funds, and other portfolio managers were looking for more yield. They hoped to not increase risk significantly because of financial regulation. Due to the Clinton era public sector surpluses the supply of government bonds was relatively scarce. Years of surpluses reduced the public debt and hence the value of outstanding government securities. In that situation, investors looked for a financial asset that was safe, liquid and had a higher return than government bonds.

Financial alchemy

Financial institutions noticed the demand for this kind of financial asset and came up with a plan. They bought mortgages from banks. These were serviced by home owners, with their homes being used as collateral. The mortgages were supposedly low risk. If home owners serviced their mortgage, banks would receive the money that was owed to them. If the home owners did not service their mortgage, banks would receive the house in order to auction it off. As real estate prices had been rising this was a situation in which banks could not lose. Wall Street banks, like Lehman Brothers, Goldman Sachs, Deutsche Bank, and the like, bought the mortgages, which were securitized. The name of the asset: mortgage—backed security (MBS). This means that the banks passed the money received from borrowers on to the holder of the MBS.

Selling single home loans in securitized form was not a viable business. Investors bought and sold financial assets worth millions or even billions. They did not deal in 100,000s of dollars. Going through the documentation of a single loan was just too much work for the buyers. They wanted to buy higher volume without having to worry much about the documentation. The Wall Street banks solved these problems by bundling the securities into what is called *Collateralized Debt Obligations* (CDOs).[5] It is like making a salami out of meat. While there is still some risk that some bad meat that went into the salami, it is quite unlikely that the whole salami will be bad. As long as real estate prices in the US did not drop in all regions at the same time, the CDOs would be considered safe. This was a convention that not many people in the markets doubted. Historically, real estate markets in the US have been regional in character. When one market went down, the other regions were not affected.

Rating agencies

The Wall Street banks used rating agencies to evaluate their CDOs. The Wall Street banks paid the rating agencies. It did not take long and the whole process degenerated into shopping for high ratings. Banks would approach rating agencies and ask them to give a rough estimate of the rating for some CDO. Rating agencies understood that if they wanted the business and the fees, they better assign a very good rating to the CDO in question. Triple A (AAA) ratings were common as rating agencies thought they had no other choice but play the game. Banks were also aware that the game would eventually blow up, but as Citibank CEO Charles "Chuck" Prince explained: "As long as the music is playing, you've got to get up and dance".[6] The banks knew that they had to sell CDOs to make the profits that other banks made. Less profits would translate into less bonus payments. As economists

---

[5] There were cases where banks sliced up CDOs and created another "salami" which was called CDO squared.

[6] https://www.reuters.com/article/financial-crisis-dancing-idUSN0819810820100408.

always say, it's about incentives, and in this case most of the incentives were skewed towards creating a bubble. The rules of the game were set up in the wrong way, and the Wall Street banks were to blame. The repeal of the 1933 Glass-Steagall Act, a main piece of legislation from the times of the Great Depression, in the 1990s was only the last step in a process of deregulation that had started in the 1980s.

Wall Street banks had now created the perfect financial asset. It was not risky, since the real estate loans were diversified (regionally). A "formula from hell" (Forbes) was used to calculate the "value"—read price—of complicated financial assets.[7] As Forbes reported, "Mr. Li's copula function rummages around in a lot of individual debt securities and then pops out one number that gives the probability of the securities all going bad at once".

For those still in doubt, the rating agencies put their rubber stamp (AAA) on the CDO. Because it was considered a super-safe asset, other banks routinely accepted CDOs as collateral. This helped potential buyers with liquidity issues.

Toxic assets and predatory lending

In the 2000s, Wall Street banks created toxic assets worth hundreds of billions of dollars. Since demand from investors was high, they had trouble finding enough mortgages to securitize. This meant that some banks specialized in lending to borrowers who were vulnerable and under normal circumstances would not qualify for a real estate loan. These banks created so-called NINJA loans: **N**o **I**ncome, **N**o **J**ob, no **A**ssets. In 2004, the FBI issued a warning that there would be widespread mortgage fraud.[8] The "epidemic" could become, according to the FBI, "the next S&L crisis".[9] The warning was ignored by the Fed, just like earlier warnings about the derivate market.

Revisiting this episode in US financial history, it is clear that banks did not serve public purpose in the years leading up to the Global Financial Crisis. Economists should have warned policymakers, the public, the press and the financial sector that something was going horribly wrong. The problem was that most economists were not paying to attention to what was going on in the banking system. They had outsourced discussions of balance sheets to the field of finance, with the result that most macroeconomists did not have and still do not have a correct understanding of money and banking. Even now,

---

[7] https://www.forbes.com/consent/ketch/?toURL=https://www.forbes.com/2009/05/07/gaussian-copula-david-x-li-opinions-columnists-risk-debt.html.
[8] https://edition.cnn.com/2004/LAW/09/17/mortgage.fraud/.
[9] The savings and loans crisis in the 1980s and 90s saw one-third of all savings and loans in the country fail.

most students of macroeconomics are taught that banks are intermediaries, lending out savings to investors. They would also borrow from the central bank and then lend on that money to households and firms, notwithstanding the fact that neither people nor firms have accounts at the Fed.[10]

In the 2003 presidential address at the meeting of the American Economists Association (AEA), economist Robert Lucas declared that the "central problem of depression-prevention has been solved, for all practical purposes, and has in fact been solved for many decades".[11] In a 2004 speech, the chairman of the Fed said: "I have argued today that improved monetary policy has likely made an important contribution not only to the reduced volatility of inflation (which is not particularly controversial) but to the reduced volatility of output as well".[12] The Fed did not see the crisis coming. There was nothing in the inflation data of the 2000s that would point to the biggest financial crisis since the Great Crash of 1929. Policymakers used the wrong models, based on faulty theory. These did not include money and banking. Up to today, these models only use money in an ad hoc manner and rely on wildly unrealistic assumptions that are mathematically convenient.

September 2008: The fall of Lehman Brothers

In summer 2007, real estate prices stopped rising in many regions of the US. This signaled trouble for the CDOs produced by Wall Street banks. What if real estate prices fell nationwide? It dawned on banks that a storm was brewing. Some of their clients started betting on a real estate crash, some—like John Paulson—bet big. Wall Street banks like Goldman Sachs realized that they still had lots of MBS in their pipeline, to be transformed into CDOs and sold off later. If the real estate market crashed, the bank would take a huge hit and might even go bankrupt. Goldman Sachs started selling these assets and buying insurance against default, mostly from AIG (American International Group). At some point, they thought that AIG would be driven into bankruptcy because they would owe Goldman Sachs lots of money in the event of a real estate crash. So, Goldman's traders started buying credit default swaps for AIG so they would still get their money.

When Goldman Sachs knew that it had hedged a good part of the risk, it started to write down the value of the assets relating to real estate. Since valuation by Goldman Sachs was seen as respectable, other banks followed in writing down their assets. Since the other banks were not hedged as well as Goldman Sachs, they experienced financial stress. When the value of assets

---

[10] https://twitter.com/federalreserve/status/1678849008574386176.
[11] https://www.aeaweb.org/articles?id=10.1257/000282803321455133.
[12] https://www.federalreserve.gov/boarddocs/speeches/2004/20040220/.

goes down, at some point total assets will be worth less than total liabilities. This would lead to technical insolvency; the Fed would have to close the bank down. Banks started frantically to sell the toxic assets that they still had on their balance sheet, but it was too late. Lehman Brothers went under in September 2008. The Fed decided to not bail out the bank, and panic followed. Other banks, like Bear Stearns, collapsed. Some were bought up by bigger banks, with the backing of the Fed.

Too-big-to-fail?

As the financial system entered in meltdown mode, policymakers started to panic. The banks communicated their problems to the policymakers. Since they owed each other billions of dollars, the insolvency of one bank would create knock-on effects on other banks. Finally, the US government decided to bail out the financial system, declaring some banks too-big-to-fail. While the decision to not let the financial system go bankrupt was sound, the idea that the government and the Fed would just support the banks with capital and liquidity while leaving the top management in power was not. Banks should have been nationalized, restructured, and either sold off to the private sector again or closed down for good if there was no viable business plan.

An alternative path to bailing out the banks would have been to declare workers too-big-to-fail. The fact that they were not able to service mortgages was the root of the financial crisis. It is not hard to understand why. In the 2000s, the US economy lost almost every third job in manufacturing. Workers struggled to make ends meet. Borrowing money to buy a house that appreciates in value seemed to be a path to prosperity, replacing the idea that work would sustain a family. Instead of bailing out the banks, the Obama administration could have increased government spending on goods and serives through massive public investment and so created employment for millions of workers who lost their jobs. This would have stabilized the price of the mortgages and eased financial troubles. Also, this would have stopped the evictions. Millions of Americans were kicked out of their flats and houses as the banks took possession.[13] That could have been avoided. The actual economic recovery from the GFC was weak. There was talk about "secular stagnation", a concept invented by Alvin Hansen in the 1930s to describe supply side factors that would impede a return of economic growth to prior levels. By now, it was clear that there had been no "secular stagnation". There was a lack of government spending, which created mass unemployment. The recent increase in government spending by the Biden administration has

---

[13] https://www.theatlantic.com/politics/archive/2016/12/obamas-failure-to-mitigate-americas-foreclosure-crisis/510485/.

shown that millions more American workers can be employed if the demand for goods and services is there.

An alternative history of the 2000s

The economic policy of the 2000s was not without alternatives. At any point, the federal government could have spent money to upgrade and build new infrastructure that is compatible with the idea of a sustainable economy. For instance, China started building its high-speed train network in 2007 and now, at 26,000 miles, has the biggest network on the planet. Also, the federal government could have invested in future technologies, ensuring that private sector firms stay in the USA and create well-paid jobs for industrial workers. The financial sector could have been regulated so that it would not wreak havoc on the economy again. The federal government could have done a lot to ensure that Americans have access to public goods and services of good quality and in good availability. My colleague Randall Wray has written a book about what the US government could do for its citizens if it wanted to (Wray 2022).

The federal government is very powerful. It can use its power to serve the interest of the few or the interests of the many. What it should do is a complicated question. There is no reason to believe that politicians are "better than us"—politicians grow up in our society and they face the same dilemmas that we are facing. We can act with the motive of self-interest, and we can act motivated by serving public purpose. We are social beings, and we need society in order to be happy. The question is what the role of government should be in our society. It should not intrude, but it should also not leave us being afraid of illness, unemployment, poverty, or discrimination of any kind. It is up for voters to decide what they want their government to do. Economists should not be in the business of telling people what is good for them. They should rather explain to citizens what is economically possible and what is not. Currently, it seems that many people don't understand the benefits of running some parts of the economy not for profit, but for the greater good of all. That does not mean that we have to move toward a different form of capitalism or any such thing. European societies, including the Scandinavian countries, have significantly bigger governments, but they are still capitalist. It would be wrong to identify more spending by the government with less capitalism. After all, the government buys lots of goods and services from private sector firms.

Understanding MMT, it becomes obvious that alternative economic policies are possible. These will be described in more detail in the next chapter.

6

Economic Policies Based on MMT

MMT is a theoretical lens through which we view the monetary system from the perspective of the state. The focus is on the use of money to provide the state with resources. MMT thereby describes how money is created and how it is removed from circulation. MMT is *not* an economic policy program. MMT cannot be "applied" or "tried out". Any ideas about how the government should conduct economic policy are not part of the core of MMT. MMT describes the accounting in the monetary system, which is explained by describing institutions with the help of balance sheets. Based on this, ideas of economic policy can be generated. Finally, we do not deal with the monetary system out of boredom, but because we think that an understanding of it can help us to solve social problems or to add new institutional building blocks that promote the public purpose. In this respect, the following ideas are *inspired* by an understanding of the monetary system in terms of MMT, but do not belong to the hard core.

One task of government economic policy is to slow down the economy in an upswing and to get it going again in a downswing. Price stability (low and stable inflation) and full employment are not automatic properties of an economy, but require deliberate regulation and policy use. The economist Hyman Minsky emphasized the economic policy of the downturn with parallel intervention by the central bank ("big bank") and the government ("big government"). This provides a good starting point.

The central bank ensures that interest rates are low and that banks remain liquid (by adequately reducing collateral standards) and the government solvent. In this way, the central bank prevents the problem of a bank run. Such an event occurs when a bank's customers have doubts about its liquidity and/or solvency. They therefore want to withdraw their money before it runs out of it. However, the central bank can lend the banks as much cash as is needed to ward off the bank run in return for collateral. In addition, the government's deposit insurance ensures that nobody loses money in a bank run. That should stop bank runs from happening.

The federal government ("big government"), on the other hand, ensures that its spending generates corresponding incomes for households and companies, which stabilizes the existing private debt structure. If households have to repay real estate loans and mortgages but cannot do so due to unemployment, the financial system will start to collapse (and ultimately require a bail-out). Thus, government spending increases incomes and employment and thus indirectly increases the sustainability of the financial system. In addition, spending generates new government bonds in which savings can be invested safely.

6.1 How Do We Ensure Full Employment?

What should a policy of demand stabilization look like? How can the state ensure both full employment and price stability? The first insight is that the change in the number of jobs in the private sector depends on whether or not firms can sell the goods and services they produce. If the consumer spending on goods and services is so high that everything can be sold, the companies will produce the same amount in the next month/quarter/year as before. New labor is not needed. If productivity increases, the same output can even be produced with less labor. But if demand is higher than supply, inventories will be emptied and some consumers will have to wait or go empty-handed. There is more demand than there is supply. Since companies usually make a profit on each item sold, they will expand production to make higher profits. A price increase would also be possible.

Conversely, demand that is below supply would lead to companies' production not being sold. That would be a problem for companies because they typically finance their production. They first spend money, which they often borrow, buy raw materials, energy, labor, and other resources and finally produce. Only then can they sell their goods and services. If they cannot sell a part of their production, they will not be able to repay their loans. They would then be forced to lower prices to increase revenues. In addition, they would produce less in the future and release workers.

Government jobs, on the other hand, are not directly dependent on the development of demand. Employees in schools, universities, the police and judiciary, the armed forces, and customs do not worry about changes in purchasing power. Fluctuations in purchasing power change the number of jobs in the private sector. If we want to achieve full employment, we have to stabilize demand (i.e., purchasing power).

Stabilizing demand

To stabilize demand, government spending and revenues (taxes) can be varied. However, since the government only determines the tax rates and not the absolute level of tax revenues, it is probably more effective to start on the expenditure side. If aggregate demand for goods and services is too low, government spending can be increased. If it is too high, the government can reduce its spending. Theoretically, tax rates can also be changed. Higher tax revenues tend to slow down the economy, while low ones speed it up.[1] However, tax increases are extremely unpopular with the entire population and therefore not a good macroeconomic policy instrument. Tax rates should be set to ensure a fair distribution of incomes and wealth.

However, there is a tendency for the existing tax system to stabilize demand. Those who earn less pay a lower average tax rate. Thus, the tax burden falls when incomes fall. This stabilizes the economy. Those who earn more during an economic boom are taxed at higher tax rates and pay more taxes. The state takes away more purchasing power. If the economy is running at full speed, tax revenues are high. If government spending is stable while the economy is red hot, this leads to the state taking more money out of the economy (via taxes) than it adds back in via its spending. The government's surplus is exactly equal to a deficit of everyone else (households, firms, and the rest of the world). All of us together pay more in taxes than we receive in government spending. This reduces our net financial assets, so demand increases less than it would without this effect. Conversely, in bad times, the government will run a deficit because tax revenues collapse (assuming constant government spending). Lower incomes lead to lower tax payments, so the public sector partially compensates for the fall in private incomes.

Automatic stabilizers

Institutional rules that stabilize demand are called automatic stabilizers. Next to the tax system the social security system is one of the automatic stabilizers. The unemployed receive unemployment benefits. This stabilizes purchasing power, which would otherwise fluctuate to a greater extent. In an ideal world, the automatic stabilizers would be sufficient to steer the economy. In times

---

[1] The effect is far from clear. Imposing tax liabilities on people might make them offer more work, as they try to stabilize their net income because they have bills to pay.

of upswing, they would automatically remove purchasing power from the economic cycle so that demand pressures do not become too great (and translate into shortages and price increases). During downturns, purchasing power would be added so that employment is stabilized.

Beyond automatic stabilizers, the government can also spontaneously increase or decrease spending. This is what we call "discretionary" economic policy, because it is the federal government itself that decides. If the automatic stabilizers are not enough to keep the economy on its path, it may enter a self-reinforcing process. Especially in a downturn, this can end badly. More unemployment leads to less demand, which in turn causes companies to reduce their production. Thus, unemployment rises and we get a downward spiral. Deflation can make everything worse, because lower prices make for lower profits. Companies that don't make profits will cut production even more. Therefore, deflation should be avoided. During an upswing an inflationary process can occur. If the supply of labor is below demand for some job categories or sectors, this can lead to strong wage growth. Companies pass on the increased costs (wages) through higher prices. Rising inflation eventually leads to higher wage demands, resulting in a vicious circle. However, we have not seen such a process in Western countries for more than half a century. (The higher inflation rates of recent years has not much to do with higher wages.)

Macroeconomic policy based on an understanding of MMT would strengthen automatic stabilizers. A Job Guarantee, discussed below, could be introduced to achieve true full employment. In addition, by bringing forward or deferring spending into the future, the government can vary its spending to stabilize demand. The Fed's task is to stabilize the interest rate, which it can easily do. For a number of years, the key interest rate was at zero. The federal government can contribute to price stability as well, which will be discussed in the next chapter.

So, in concrete terms, one (of many possible) MMT-based economic policies would be that in times of excessively high demand, the government shifts its spending into the future (to free resources that are needed in other parts of the economy) and tries to limit wage growth, e.g., by raising the wages of government sector employees at a weaker rate than before. Similarly, the government can intervene by changing the regulation of banks, restricting credit creation in areas of the economy that are "running hot". It can also take other measures that cause citizens to spend less money today. For example, it can raise prices for services it provides (public transport, railroads, outdoor swimming pools, etc.). The important thing is to find the source of the inflation problem, which then requires a specific solution tailored to that source.

A one-size-fits-all solution is unlikely to work and might even make the rise in the consumer price level worse.

Unemployment in figures

Unemployment is measured in absolute terms or as a share of the employed population. However, the corresponding statistics are subject to interpretation and should be treated with caution. Government authorities use them to provide the state with a report card on its economic policy, so they have an incentive to tamper with the data. An objective indicator of full employment would be a sharp rise in labor income when companies compete for workers. Figure 6.1 shows the reasons for unemployment in 2022. With millions unemployed permanently, we are not even close to full employment. Though no every unemployed worker is involuntary, it must be assumed that the majority is.

Figure 6.2 shows that the employment to population ratio was higher in the 1990s than it is today, both for the general public and for females aged 25–54. In an aging society we would expect to see the ratio falling, but the fall during the pandemic and the subsequent rise have shown that there is no autopilot here which somehow returns the employment ratio to its optimum. Obviously, it is not the goal of economic policy to employ everyone. Not all citizens want to work. Some cannot because they are ill, others are either too

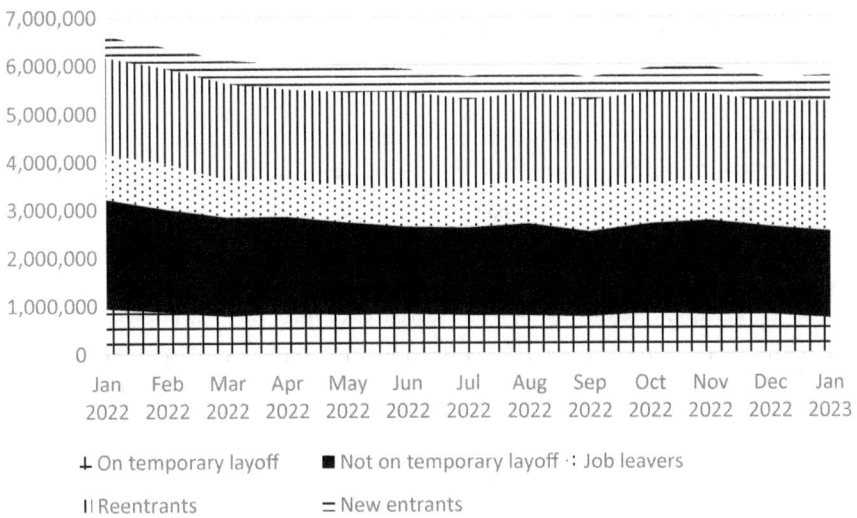

Fig. 6.1 Reasons for unemployment, January 2022–January 2023, millions. *Source* Bureau of Labor Statistics, U.S. Department of Labor, The Economics Daily, Number of unemployed at 5.7 million in January 2023 at https://www.bls.gov/opub/ted/2023/number-of-unemployed-at-5-7-million-in-january-2023.htm (visited February 09, 2023)

Fig. 6.2 General employment to population ratio (black) and employment to population ratio for females aged 25–54, quarterly data. *Sources* BLS (LNS12300000) and OECD (LREM25FE)

young or too old, and still others don't want to work because they don't need to.

When looking at unemployment, the unemployment rate alone is not enough. The employment to population ratio sometimes provides us with a much clearer picture of what is going on. We should also examine measures of underemployment as there are certainly more workers available if only more and better job would be offered. There are also millions of part-time workers who would prefer to work full-time.

6.2 How Do We Ensure Price Stability?

The inflation rate measures the change in prices of consumer goods, taken from a certain chosen basket of goods. If the price of a basket of consumer goods increases we talk about inflation. If the price of the basket of goods falls, we experience deflation.

Since many products are subject to technological development, the price statistics do not always reflect actual prices, but rather prices reduced by the estimated technical advantage—this statistic should be treated with caution, e.g., with regard to the actual additional burden of price increases on households. It is an average that is not suitable for reflecting the actual change in the purchasing power of all individual households. Next to the unemployment rate the inflation rate is usually a standard target of economic policy.

It is important to realize that the increase of just one price does not mean that the inflation rate rises. Another consumer good might have been reduced in price. Thus, if butter becomes more expensive, it may well be that apples become cheaper at the same time, leaving the price of the basket unchanged. Prices are made by companies and are based on costs. Depending on the situation, the companies may allow themselves to add a certain profit markup to their costs to determine their price.[2]

At this point, we can note that price changes are mostlyly consequences of changes of costs. In particular, the costs of labor—salaries and wages—and energy—electricity, oil, and gas—are reflected in prices. When these costs rise, companies can either earn less while keeping prices the same, or they can raise prices to stabilize profits. Normally, companies do the latter, since they have to pay off debts and interest on an ongoing basis and a reduction in profits can lead to all sorts of nasty side effects (higher interest rates, lower share prices, etc.).

Inflation

Inflation arises for various reasons. In modern industrialized societies it arises, among other things, when wages grow faster than productivity. (This means that unit labor costs rise.) Roughly speaking, the rise in unit labor costs, the excess of wage growth over productivity growth, and the rate of inflation are often very similar and have the same turning points. However, prices can also rise when firms exploit their market power. This is the case, for example, when pharmaceutical companies increase their prices because they have little or no competition and regulation does not prohibit them from doing so.

Figure 6.3 shows the inflation rate (black line) and the change in unit labor costs (dashed line). The difference between the two fluctuates around zero. It rarely exceeds + 2 and − 2%. The change in unit labor costs is therefore a good approximation of the inflation rate. The logic here runs as follows: if wages grow faster than productivity, then wage earners' spending grows faster than the size of the pie (GDP). If the latter grows by 2%, but wages grow by 4% on average, then firms would be able to raise prices by 2% and still sell everything. On average and over time, this describes relatively accurately the rate of inflation.

It is interesting to know where the price level comes from in the first place. Why does a coffee cost three dollars and not one hundred or one thousand dollars? In Italy, when they had the lira instead of the euro, an espresso cost about a thousand lira. Why is it only two euros today? It is clear that the number following the currency unit says nothing about whether a good is expensive or cheap. In order to estimate the purchasing power, we need to know how easy or hard it is to get the currency.

If workers were earning 1.5 currency units per hour, we would expect different prices in the economy than if workers earned 8000 currency units

---

[2] Firms adjust prices only very rarely, just as prices on the menu of a restaurant though prices of ingredients will vary daily.

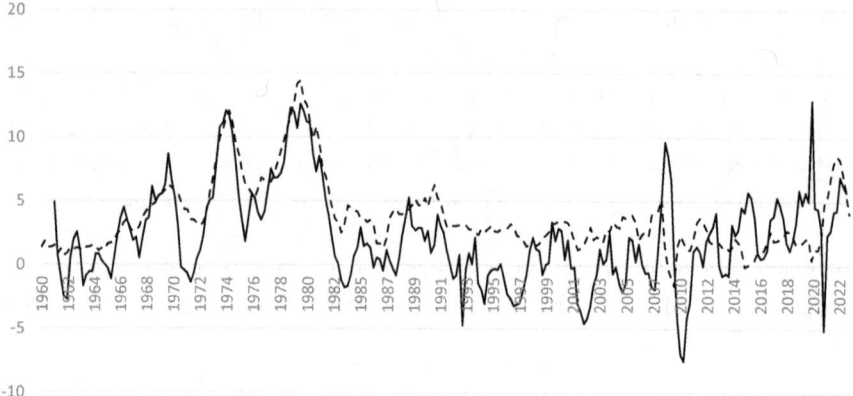

Fig. 6.3 Change in unit labor costs (striped) and inflation (black line), in percent. *Sources* OECD (LCULMN01USQ661S) and BLS (CPIAUCSL)

per hour. In essence it is the fixing of wages in the currency unit that anchors the price level of a currency. The state plays a major role here by paying wages of its public sector employees. Companies have to offer higher wages to convince employees to work in the private sector. While the state offers permanent employment, jobs in private companies are always fraught with uncertainty. Firms can go bankrupt and then the job would be gone.

Companies can borrow money and pay higher wages by taking on more debt, but in the long term this must also lead to higher profits. If it doesn't, companies will lower wages to a level at which they expect to make profits. One problem with private sector wages that are too high would be that the government would draw more and more money out of circulation via constantly rising tax revenues, which would then no longer be available to the companies as profit. The state has an important say in wage increases by determining the salaries and wages of state employees.

Generating price stability

As we have seen, the inflation rate over the decades depends essentially on the change in unit labor costs. Government spending can cause wages to rise faster, which helps to hit the inflation target of two percent over the long run, as defined by the Fed. Where the government hires additional labor, labor may become scarce. The government can then only hire additional workers if it outbids wages offered by the private sector. If this happens on a large scale, this can have an inflationary effect. This is especially relevant when wages for low-skilled labor rise and other sectors are forced to raise their own wages in order to avoid a migration of their workers to other sectors. Companies can cope with higher wages—they simply raise prices. When all firms do that, we see higher inflation.

The government can also directly influence wages, as it is also an employer in the public sector. If it enforces wage increases that are higher than the average of recent years, then the rate of inflation will tend to rise (and the reverse). In addition, the state can influence the inflation rate through public sector prices, for example, when it increases museum admission prices, social insurance contributions, vehicle taxes, or other prices.

Here, too, it is important to realize that the state only needs money to move resources. If individual prices go up, then the state can influence the supply of goods and services or available labor. For example, if engineers are in short supply, the state can spend money on additional study places and thus reduce wage pressure in the medium term. Wages and prices are indicators of scarcity in some sectors of the economy, but the scarcity is a supply side problem. When it comes to scarcity of certain workers in a sector, it can be eliminated by appropriate education policies.

Energy prices and inflation

A very important price for the US economy is the price of oil. Oil enters into the production process in many sectors. We also run most of our cars with gasoline, which is processed oil. Any increase in the price of oil will increase the costs in many sectors of the US economy. This will very likely lead to higher prices as firms are likely to shift the burden of higher costs toward the consumer. Since there is no readily available substitute for oil, firms and households will consume more or less the same quantity of oil even if prices are increasing. This is why a rise in the oil price can also increase the rate of inflation. Figure 6.4 reveals two episodes when this happened. One was just prior to the Global Financial Crisis in 2007 and the other during the pandemic, starting in 2020.

Any increase in costs could theoretically lead firms to increase prices. However, energy costs and labor costs are probably the biggest cost factors of the US economy. There are also other inputs that can drive inflation, like medicine, college tuition, or used cars. While periods of low inflation are usually quite alike, periods of high inflation need to be analyzed in detail because these periods are not alike.

Resources and spending

In macroeconomic terms, rising prices and wages will lead to more money being spent. Since prices always include a share of taxes—including the value-added tax—tax revenues will rise. This automatically withdraws money from

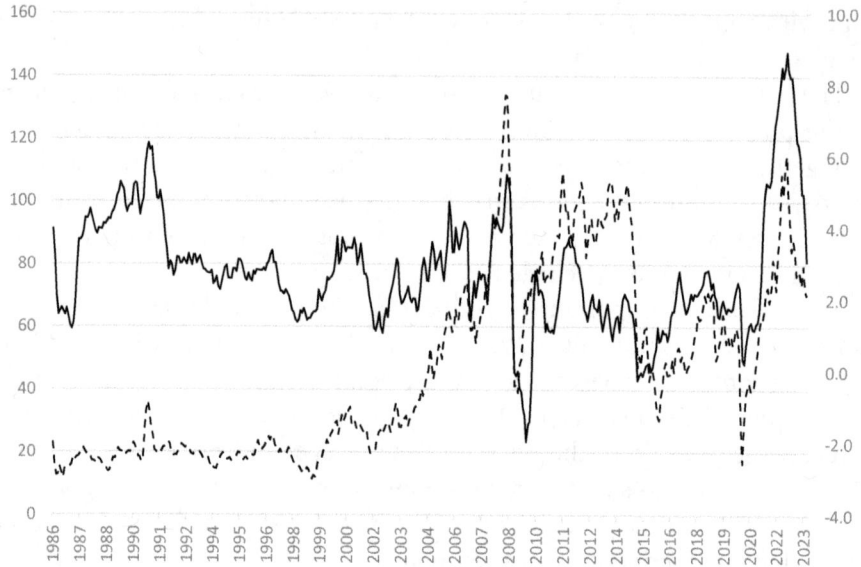

Fig. 6.4 Oil price (striped, LHS) and rate of inflation (black, RHS), in USD per barrel and percent. *Sources* U.S. Energy Information Administration [DCOILWTICO] and BLS [CPIAUCSL]

households and companies when the inflation rate rises in an upswing. At the same time, government payments under the social security system fall in good times and rise in bad times. Rising household incomes and increasing corporate profits also lead to more money being paid to the state. Since the federal government sets its expenditures independently of revenues (which are only generated in the course of the year), there will be lower government deficits or even (rising) surpluses. As a result, purchasing power will be reduced and demand for goods will fall. Thus, production will decrease as well as the demand for labor. Ultimately, this will put an end to the high wage increases.

In his 1940 book "How to Pay for the War", the English economist John Maynard Keynes described the alternatives available to England in the war economy. Since resources had to be diverted from the production of consumer goods to be used in the production of war goods, mass purchasing power needed to be reduced to free resources for the government. If this was not done, the English people would find that they could not buy the consumption goods with their old incomes. The quantity of consumption goods needed to be greatly reduced. This problem affects us when we transform our societies to fight climate change. If we need resources for a Green New Deal (GND), they will have to come from somewhere. Initially, the unemployed can be hired, but at some point, it will be necessary to divert labor from other sectors.

Taxes and government bonds as alternatives in controlling inflation

If the government attracts more workers by offering higher wages, companies will have to raise wages to keep their workers on the job and happy. They will then raise prices of their goods and services and higher inflation will follow. It would be more efficient to use the two instruments of taxes and government bonds to keep inflation rates more or less constant. Taxes directly reduce the purchasing power of those taxed, thus freeing up resources that can be bought by the state at a reasonable price. However, higher taxes are usually perceived (at least in part rightly) as appropriation, and many people do not like this. Therefore, the second option could be more acceptable, reducing purchasing power today by promising more purchasing power tomorrow.

If citizens use a part of their income to buy interest-bearing government bonds this ensures that income is set aside, thus freeing up resources. The restrictions on consumption today are then combined with an increase in consumption tomorrow. For those affected, this would be a much more pleasant perspective than depriving them of income for good through additional taxes and higher tax rates.[3]

The government can also fight inflation by imposing bans. It can remove from the economy goods whose consumption is undesirable. For example, after a future expansion of the Amtrak rail network that turns it into a continental high-speed rail network, domestic flights could be banned outright instead of taxed. With taxation, the price of flights would rise, which would tend to increase inflation. With the ban, domestic flights are removed from the consumer price index altogether, leaving the price level unchanged.

The government can also significantly reduce the price of local public transportation, for example, by introducing low-cost $365 tickets valid for one year.[4] Or it can reduce tax rates in sectors that operate CO_2-neutral. Or it could provide goods free of charge that displace scarce and costly private goods. This could come into play in the housing market, for example. If the state were to build municipal housing on a large scale it would bring down rents. It is important not to create additional consumption by lowering prices. This would increase the quantity of consumer goods produced and hence have a counterproductive effect.

---

[3] Obviously, one would have to assure that when consumption increases in the future, there must be a supply of goods and services available to be purchased at stable prices.

[4] In the meantime, the German government has created a public transport ticket valid for one month in all of Germany at the price of 9 euros.

6.3 The Job Guarantee

The federal government, as the creator of money, can put any desired quantity of its currency into circulation as long as its citizens are willing and able to sell labor, goods and services, or other assets to the government. It does not "cost" anything in monetary terms. It follows that involuntary unemployment has a simple remedy. The federal government simply spends more money. The increase in spending creates more jobs in the public and private sector. The government decides on the actual distribution, and we as voters can let our politicians know about the distribution we prefer. However, government spending and tax rates are unlikely to create a demand for goods and services such that everybody who wants to work finds a job. So, a few people will be involuntarily unemployed. This is where the Job Guarantee (JG) comes in.[5]

The idea is that the federal government will provide the involuntarily unemployed with the additional option of getting a job oriented toward the public purpose. It pays a fair wage that allows for a good life. Currently, $15 per hour plus social security benefits is being discussed. A Job Guarantee job is available to anyone who can and wants to work but cannot find employment. No one is required to take up a job as all other social benefits are left in place. Work in the Job Guarantee sector should not compete with regular jobs in the private and public sectors. At the municipal level, this could be monitored by a committee made up of representatives from politics, employer associations, unions and civil society. This body would also ensure that a large number of jobs with different tasks is always available. This gives job seekers the opportunity to find a job that suits them. Some of the jobs will be designed in such a way that it is also possible to work half days or other hours that suit potential job candidates.

JG jobs will be treated no differently than other jobs. Those who do not show up for work or are consistently late will be laid off. Those who fail to meet expectations, are misbehaving or breaking the rules will be laid off. In addition to these duties there are also rights, namely the right to hold a permanent job. Job security and the freedom of JG workers are increased. The long-term goal of the JG is for workers to find their way back into "normal" employment. Since higher wages are paid in both private and public sectors, there is a strong incentive for people with JG jobs to leave the JG program as soon as possible. Companies will be pleased that they can now hire workers

---

[5] See Tcherneva (2020), Forstater and Murray (2013), and Ehnts and Höfgen (2019).

from the JG instead of having to hire from the pool of the long-term unemployed. This makes companies more flexible and enables them to create and fill productive jobs more easily and in greater numbers, especially during an upswing.

The JG thus acts as an automatic stabilizer. In bad times, it catches the unfortunates who are affected by rising unemployment. This means that their income does not fall back to unemployment benefits and later to social security, but they can stabilize their income at a higher level. This will also stabilize demand for goods and services. Companies will lay off fewer workers in recessions or depressions. Prices will remain more stable as companies can now sell more at given prices. They are not forced to cut prices as quickly. In turn, incomes rise less during an upswing. Somebody moving from unemployment to employment has a much higher increase in income than someone moving from the JG to employment. As a result, the increase in demand is smaller in the upswing, which means that inflation will be stabilized. The Job Guarantee thus practically eliminates involuntary unemployment.

The JG will also raise wages at the bottom end, since it will act as a de facto federal minimum wage. If citizens can chose between a private sector job at $7.25, which is the minimum wage in many states, and a $15 JG job, most will opt for the latter. This decreases inequality and the personal and social ills that come with it. It also improves the economy because higher wages lead to more demand for goods and services. Given that there is still some significant under- and unemployment, the economy might still expand and employment with it. Obviously, the government has to ensure that this does not lead to further degradation of the environment and resource and energy use that is incompatible with the 2016 Paris Agreement on climate change.

The JG will thus improve the bargaining situation for those citizens with the lowest incomes, which should be a good thing. Companies are constantly competing, which puts them under pressure. They are forced to have competitive prices; otherwise their sales and market share will decline. What should happen is that companies increase productivity in order to compete. They can thus afford to pay higher nominal wages while cutting their average costs. If productivity grows at 5%, for instance, then wages can be increased by that rate plus the inflation target, which usually is assumed to be roughly 2%. Things will work out for the private sector as a whole as the wages paid to workers return in the form of revenues when workers spend their income as consumers.

An alternative way to stay competitive is to rely on cheap labor and not invest in higher productivity. That way, firms will be able to keep up their profits and their market share at the cost of the workers. At the sectoral level, this will lead to macroeconomic problems as the low wages do not create the purchasing power needed for the sale of the output. While firms on average will do well, some will be struggling. Increasing debt might result, as firms that are not profitable survive by borrowing from financial markets. This increases financial fragility and the risk of a big financial crisis in the future.

6.4 Industrial Policy

Industrial policy has made a comeback in recent years. There is growing recognition that the US has lost millions of manufacturing jobs in the first decade of this century (see Fig. 6.5). In order to increase the number of good jobs (well-paying and probably unionized), the federal government has vowed to bring back jobs in the automotive and chips sectors. This goes hand in hand with anti-Chinese rhetoric. China has been flagged as a threat to US national economic interests, and there is now significant momentum to reduce dependency on Chinese technology. The Russian attack on Ukraine has also highlighted the uncertainty surrounded any trade with Taiwan, an island adjacent to the Chinese mainland that is claimed by the People's Republic as their territory.

The discussion of industrial policy has to start with supply side considerations. Why is it that almost all consumer electronics are produced in Asia? The reason lies in the way that production is structured. Electronics production is dominated by very large factories with very expensive machinery, like robots. They produce a lot of output, and this is why they have low costs. They run the machinery 24 h a day on 365 days a year. Smaller factories

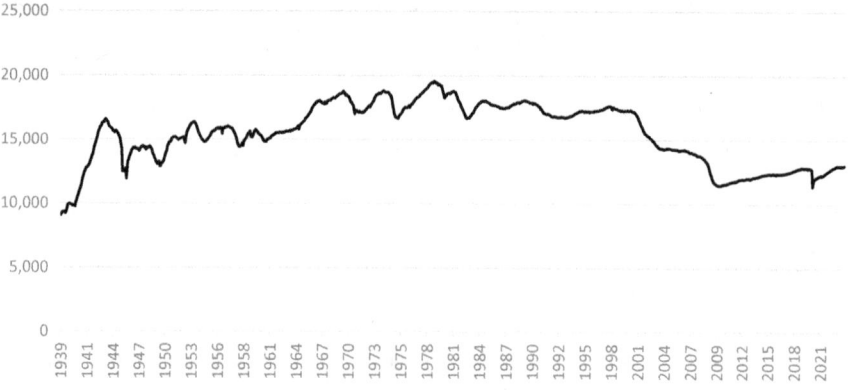

Fig. 6.5 Employees in manufacturing, thousands of persons, seasonally adjusted. *Source* BLS via FRED https://fred.stlouisfed.org/series/MANEMP

would not be able to compete since lower output means less machinery and hence higher costs. This is what economists call increasing returns to scale. It is a property of most industrial production. It means that when firms compete, the big ones will win and get bigger. This process can lead to a monopoly held by the surviving firm. A monopoly is the most cost-effective way of production, but it gives the producer too much power—there are no competitors. The producer could just raise prices and thus increase profits. Consumers have no alternatives, and firms will not jump into the sector because they know that the monopolist can bring prices down any time to get rid of unwanted competition.

Inflation Reduction Act

The Inflation Reduction Act includes a lot of spending, including subsidies for firms located in the US (like producers of electric cars) that use local components (like batteries). It also requires firms to create well-paying jobs that are unionized. It is designed to grow the economy "from the bottom up".[6] In terms of economic costs, there is definitely a trade-off between costs and access. In some sectors, the rest of the world produces more cheaply than US firms. That is not a problem as long as:

1. The firms are selling to the USA without restrictions.
2. The firms are accepting US dollars.

The first issue that might arise is that US consumers and firms lose access to goods and services they want or need for production of other goods and services. This would leave them dependent on possibly unreliable partners, especially state-run companies in countries that are politically unfriendly or even hostile to the US. It is more of a strategic issue than a cost issue. It is quite similar to agricultural subsidies, where the main argument is that the US should not have to rely on food imports because it might easily be blackmailed. To run the US economy, there are certain goods and services that are crucial and, in the short run, irreplaceable. Communications infrastructure, for instance, should be built in a way that ensures it can always be maintained, even if economic relations between the USA and some of the supplying countries break down completely.

The second argument is that firms are willing to the sell against US dollars. It is a great advantage for consumers and firms to be able to use US dollars to buy goods and services from the rest of the world. Other countries would

---

[6] https://www.whitehouse.gov/briefing-room/statements-releases/2022/08/19/fact-sheet-the-inflation-reduction-act-supports-workers-and-families/.

need to earn or borrow US dollars *before* they can buy—not so for the US. While this point is not as important as the first point, it is a point of strategic concern. US firms and consumers would be limited in their purchases of foreign goods and services if these were invoiced in foreign currency. The US dollar will be the world currency of the decades to come as hundreds of billions of debts denominated in US dollars exist.

Public or private employment?

The federal government can choose to subsidize private employment in the manufacturing sector, but it might as well follow the example of other countries and create more manufacturing jobs. For instance, it could upgrade its high-speed rail network through having Amtrak spend billions on trains and infrastructure. It could invest billions in infrastructure that charges electric vehicles at competitive prices for everybody.[7] It could upgrade public colleges and universities so that they offer better education for free, like in many European countries. It could create institutions that help private sector companies with research and development, like Germany does with its Fraunhofer institutes. These expenditures are not counted as subsidies and are compatible with the rules of the World Trade Organization. Any expansion of public workers in manufacturing will very likely lead to an increase in the number of private workers in manufacturing. Any significant industrial policy should be part of a Green New Deal.

6.5 A Green New Deal

The environmental and social problems that we perceive today are the result of political decisions made in the past. Inequality is at record levels in many countries. Likewise, the average temperature rise on our planet should give pause for thought. What can we do now? What options do we have to address the problems? What tools do we have at our disposal? How do we change the current results of economic activity?

Two problems stand out. First, the economic gains are distributed very unevenly. Figure 6.6 shows that the share of total income going to the top 1% of income earners has increased from 10% around 1980 to almost 20%, almost doubling over the last four decades. The share of the lower 50% (not shown) has fallen from about 20% to less than 15%. This means that

---

[7] Currently, some (super)chargers are only available to customers from one car producer, which is an inefficient arrangement. Also, private companies running chargers might overcharge clients, which oftentimes have no option of not charging when their battery is very low.

economic growth has lifted mostly the boats of the relatively wealthy, leaving half of the US population relatively worse off. Any Green New Deal worth the name should ensure that the gap between the incomes at the top and the bottom is closing. If instead the economic costs are dumped on the lower half of income earners, this will be unjust and lead to more disruptive politics.

The other problem is climate change itself. As Fig. 6.7 shows, global average temperatures have been rising over recent decades. Since 1980 the rate of increase has risen. By now it is uncontroversial that we are the drivers of climate change. Our emissions warm up the planet, threatening to heat it up in a way that is destructive to most life forms. The heat wave that gripped Western North America in 2023 is one of the worst on record, and this is only the beginning. As the planet heats up, we will suffer more from cardiovascular diseases. These are the leading causes of death globally, with 17.9 million lives taken annually according to the World Health Organization.[8] There is no easy fix to this.

Economist William Nordhaus claims that the US economy will not be affected much by climate change because we mostly work indoors. Air-conditioning would "fix" climate change. As Keen (2021) argues, that view is hopelessly naïve. While agriculture might represent a small share of GDP, any larger problems in the food supply will feed through to the rest of the economy. Also, there are breaking points in some of nature's systems, like the Gulf Stream, that are very hard to predict. Last but not least it is unclear where we get our energy from if we can't continue to use fossil fuels. So, there is plenty to worry about.

Fig. 6.6 Share of the top 1% in total income. *Source* WID

---

[8] https://www.who.int/health-topics/cardiovascular-diseases#tab=tab_1.

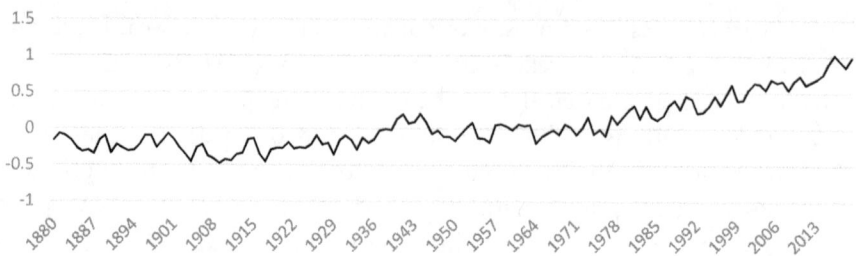

Fig. 6.7 Global average temperature 1880–2019. *Source* GISTEMP Team, 2020: GISS Surface Temperature Analysis (GISTEMP), version 4. NASA Goddard Institute for Space Studies

The good news is that the social and ecological transformation of society will not fail because of money. After all, money is not limited and can be created free of charge in banks and central banks. What is limited, however, are resources. These resources can be allocated to the desired uses.

We can buy everything we need for a Green New Deal: labor, goods and services, means of production, patents, land and real estate, even stocks, and companies.

Public purpose or profit?

In short, there are essentially two ways we can use money to move resources. The first way is the generation of money by the state. The state can then spend the money with the public purpose in mind, year after year. The federal government does not have to "fund itself", but simply spends money that is newly created. It can therefore use resources as it sees fit without running out of money. Elections ensure that the federal government does not use or even waste resources for the benefit of a few.

The government has the public purpose in mind when it spends. It does not have to make a profit and is free to budget expenditures year after year. The decisions on spending are made by politicians. For example, elementary schools are run even though they do not generate a profit. However, there is a social consensus that citizens should be educated, and this begins in the elementary school if not in kindergarten. The school receives money from the state to maintain its buildings, to pay teachers and staff, to pay for materials, and whatever other monetary costs arise.

Competition plays little or no role here. Schools are not supposed to work by cutting costs in order to maximize profits, because it can be assumed that the quality of the "services" (teaching) offered would then be reduced. In addition, competition would lead to above-average schools becoming larger and larger, while below-average schools would shrink and eventually disappear. This would mean that the supply of elementary schools in the area would no longer be guaranteed. In some cases, children would have to be driven for hours to attend a school. It would make little sense.

The state does not have to shy away from uncertainty in its spending. It may not be clear, for example, where the price of electricity will be in 2040. This would be important for decisions for or against the construction of power plants, grid lines, or batteries. Private companies might therefore refrain from investing, as the potential profits would not be clear. The state, on the other hand, can still invest. This gives it a clear advantage over private companies when it comes to long-term investments in infrastructure.

The second way of using money to move resources is the capitalist method. The idea is very simple but powerful. A company raises money, either by issuing shares or securities or by borrowing or mining its own assets. The purpose of doing business is to make a profit, from which interest or dividends are then paid. Companies that can pay their interest/dividends will stabilize or even reduce their indebtedness. Companies that cannot pay their interest/dividends due to insufficient profits must increase their indebtedness and rely on the financial markets to allow them to do so. If this does not happen, they are forced out of the market.

This way of doing business is not aimed directly at the public purpose, but at (private) profits. This can be unproblematic, but it does not have to be. Adam Smith is known to have thought about the coincidence of public purpose and profits. Ideally, the invisible hand should bring the two into harmony. However, we see today that when private profits are made, the public purpose is sometimes very clearly not served.

In many profitable economic activities, for example, the environment is polluted or wages and incomes are generated that are incompatible with the public purpose. This includes excessive managerial salaries as well as (illegal) low wages paid below the minimum wage. A major environmental problem is CO_2 emissions. The costs to society are not imposed on the company, which allows it to continue to make high profits.

Private companies in transition

There is also dissatisfaction in the automotive industry. Internal combustion engines generate noise and exhaust fumes, resulting in thousands of additional deaths every year. At the same time, the problem with electric cars is that there is still no adequate charging infrastructure and the electric cars are relatively expensive. There is no agreement even on the standards. Moreover, it is not clear whether the ecological footprint of electric cars is really as good as claimed.

At this point, the state is called upon to enforce the public purpose. On the one hand, it can force companies to focus more on the public purpose through more effective regulation. The proposals of the common good economy also go in this direction. The idea is that companies should draw up balance sheets that show the impact of their activities on the common good.

However, this alone will not be sufficient for social and environmental change, because the future of infrastructure is fraught with uncertainty. Companies simply do not know what the world will look like in 30 years and whether long-term investments in charging infrastructure, for example, will be worthwhile. This is where the entrepreneurial state (Marianna Mazzucato) needs to take action and lead the way through invention and innovation, as well as building infrastructure. There will be no problems with financing—the state simply needs to increase its spending.

Money is not the problem

If political hurdles stand in the way of any additional spending by the state, they must be circumvented. The debt ceiling, for instance, does not make any economic sense. Why not let the federal government spend more money if American workers have expressed their wish to see this government in power? Why follow rules like CUTGO, the cut-as-you-go rule that requires any increase in government spending to be at least partly financed through cuts in spending elsewhere (or increases in tax revenues)? The federal government should spend money to fix the deficits of the society, not to hit some random and nonsensical number for the public deficit or public debt.

We could create an American Investment Bank (AIB) as a vehicle to deliver the Green New Deal.[9] The idea is the following. The AIB sells green bonds to investors, raising money. It disburses this money to state and local governments, which then spend the money on the Green New Deal. They pay interest on the bonds. State and local governments are allowed to draw $2500 (or $1000) per citizen per year through green bonds until pre-determined climate targets are met. The maturity of the green bonds is 25 years. In 2049, voters can then decide whether to replace the green bonds with new (green) bonds or to pay them off using a different financial arrangement.

The Fed would be empowered to take over market management for the green bonds. It would buy and sell these bonds in such a way that their price (and hence their yield) is as stable as possible. It thus acts as a dealer of last

---

[9] A (private) bank of that name existed until 2005.

resort, ensuring there is ample liquidity and no default risk. The bottom line is that investors will know they can always sell to the Fed at a good price. Therefore, green bonds will always be in high demand. The interest rate on the bonds is based on the Fed's key interest rates, so they do not lose their appeal even if the policy rate changes in the future.

If state and local governments then spend additional dollars, part of these will flow back as tax revenue. This means that state and local governments expand their opportunities to use resources for the public purpose. They can reduce their state debts and spend wisely, with voters punishing those governments that cannot or do not want to use the money to put resources to good use.

Reducing working hours

An essential policy instrument of a socio-ecological transformation is certainly the limitation of weekly working hours. Currently, it is around 39 h per week. However, since the resulting consumption leads to a consumption of raw materials and energy that is not sustainable, we need to reduce working hours in order to reduce the supply of goods. We could start with the 4-day week. This leaves more time for family, friends, leisure, and perhaps politics and activism as well as education, culture, and travel.

Historically, we have reduced working hours' time and time again. In 1800s, many Americans worked seventy hours or more per week. By the 1900, this number was down to about sixty hours a week. Today, we are at forty hours a week, though many workers work overtime. Companies have agreed to the reductions in working hours over the last 200 years. After all, the productivity of workers has increased.

If we have already gone from sixty working hours per week in 1900 to forty working hours in 2020, why shouldn't we be able to reduce even more? Of course, we will then produce less and consume less, but that is precisely the goal! The quality of life would probably still increase for most people. Improved quality of life does not always require expensive consumption, but rather free time in the first place. In addition, the consumption is not reduced to zero but only lowered. A bicycle tour with a delicious ice cream at a stop in between will still be possible.

6.6 Inequality and Climate Justice

Climate change can only be limited if we limit the emission of greenhouse gases (including CO_2) and ultimately reduce net emissions to zero in the long term. This means that as many greenhouse gases must be absorbed as are emitted. Since we are currently emitting far more greenhouse gases than the earth is absorbing, this means that we will have to emit fewer greenhouse gases in the future than we do today—significantly fewer. The transformation of the economy takes time. (Carbon Capture and Storage does not seem to be factor in the coming decades from today's perspective.)

So far, we have assumed that we can follow an adjustment path as described in Fig. 6.8. The 2012 data show the baseline scenario, in which no adaptation takes place. Here, climate change is ignored, and companies do not change their technologies or production levels.

The 450-ppm target can only be achieved if we reduce net emissions to zero by 2100. The unit ppm measures the carbon dioxide content in the air, and emissions are measured in gigatons of CO_2 equivalents. However, by 2020, we were still on the path of the baseline scenario. From now on, the adaptation path will have to be much steeper, i.e., we will have to cut CO_2 emissions faster and more strongly if we want to stop the earth from warming by more than 1.5–2 °C until 2100.

Where do the emissions come from?

We can only achieve lower emissions if we shape consumption differently. In particular, we need to move away from fossil fuels. These are not so easy to replace, however, because wind energy, solar energy, and hydroelectric energy are firstly not yet fully developed, secondly dependent on wind, sun, and water, and thirdly not necessarily available where industry is located. Either

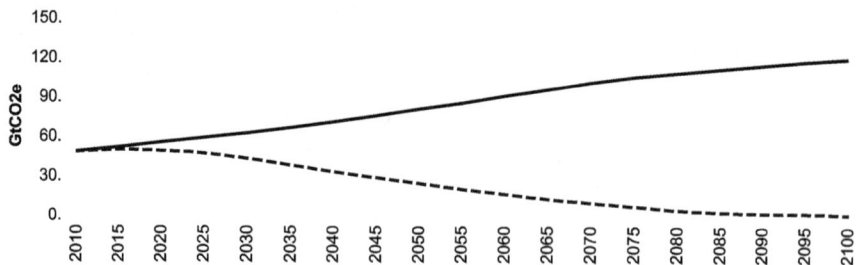

Fig. 6.8 Alternative emission paths (from 2012), base case, and 450-ppm target (dashed) annual net emissions in $GtCO_2e$. *Source* https://www.oecd.org/environment/cop21-climate-change-in-figures.htm

new power lines have to be built or companies have to relocate to where the power is generated.

In 2017, the Carbon Disclosure Project (CDP) found that just 100 companies are responsible for over 70% of industrial greenhouse gas emissions since 1988.[10] Half of these greenhouse gas emissions come from just 25 companies. It is also interesting to note that we emitted more greenhouse gases in the 28 years from 1988 to 2016 than we did in the 237 years prior to 1988. Since the beginning of the Industrial Revolution, more than half of the emissions have been caused by just 100 companies. Global warming is therefore a consequence of the industrial activities of these companies. Our past and present consumption of the goods they produce is warming up the planet.

Emissions and distribution

Figure 6.9 illustrates that the lifestyle of high-income people is the main problem. Half of the people with the highest incomes are responsible for about 90% of the emissions caused by their lifestyle, while the lowest 50% are responsible for only 10%. Of course, this does not mean that they are the better people (which could still be true), but rather that they do not have the opportunity to shape their lifestyles in a way that produces (too) many emissions.

However, we can also see that we need to adjust the ecological footprint significantly in the direction of lower-income people. This insight is politically sensitive. Who would want to tell voters that they should tighten their belts in the future?

Fig. 6.9 Share of emissions caused by lifestyle from deciles ranked by income. *Source* Oxfam (https://oi-files-d8-prod.s3.eu-west-2.amazonaws.com/s3fs-public/file_attachments/mb-extreme-carbon-inequality-021215-en.pdf)

---

[10] https://www.theguardian.com/sustainable-business/2017/jul/10/100-fossil-fuel-companies-investors-responsible-71-global-emissions-cdp-study-climate-change.

Tackling climate change should therefore always be done with distribution in mind. It would make sense to reduce consumption where it occurs. It would make little sense to penalize the less well-off through taxes on gasoline or energy. This would lead to social tensions, as we have seen in France in recent years. There, the yellow vests movement is fighting against taxes that make their commute to work more expensive and thus reduces their meager income. The rich will hardly notice whether gasoline has become more expensive or not. A political decision must be made on how to distribute the costs. Costs are to be interpreted here as a loss of consumption. This does not necessarily mean that incomes will fall or taxes will be levied by the same amount (measured in dollars in each case).

6.7 An Economic Bill of Rights for the Twenty-First Century

Alan Minsky, Executive Director of Progressive Democrats of America (PDA), and Professor Harvey J. Kaye have authored an economic bill of rights. It is inspired by the Second Bill of Rights, as proposed by Franklin Delano Roosevelt (FDR) in 1944. The twenty-first century economic bill of rights would establish that all Americans have a right to[11]:

1. A useful job that pays a living wage.
2. A voice in the workplace through a union and collective bargaining.
3. Comprehensive quality health care.
4. Complete cost-free public education and access to broadband internet.
5. Decent, safe, affordable housing.
6. A clean environment and a healthy planet.
7. A meaningful endowment of resources at birth, and a secure retirement.
8. Sound banking and financial services.
9. An equitable and economically fair justice system.
10. Recreation and participation in civic and democratic life.

The idea that Americans have economic rights is sound. It links to the United States Bill of Rights, which comprises the first ten amendments to the United States Constitution. Citizens do not only have *negative* rights, protecting them from other citizens or an overreaching state, but also *positive* rights, which are mostly economic and social rights. These rights should start

---

[11] https://www.commondreams.org/views/2022/04/25/time-has-come-progressives-rescue-and-renew-american-democracy.

with the right to work, which should pay living wage. Work is still crucial in the twenty-first century. Workers should have a say in the workplace. It helps increase productivity and stops workers from being exploited. Quality health care should be a right as well. Spending on health care in the US is much higher than anywhere, but average life expectancy in the USA is less than in many other developed countries. Currently, life expectancy is falling because of the pandemic.[12]

Can the US provide its citizens with quality health care, broadband internet, free public education, and affordable housing? The answer does not depend on whether we can find the money to pay for it. What matters is the availability of resources. Are there enough doctors, nurses, hospitals, and emergency rooms? Is there enough communications infrastructure? Are there enough professors, teaching assistants, and buildings to provide free education? Is there enough housing, both private and public, to ensure that it is affordable? If there are not enough resources, can we supply more resources? If so, we can afford all these things.

Can we afford a clean environment and a healthy planet? I guess that we cannot afford to have a dirty environment and a frail planet. The costs of climate change and a polluted environment would be very high, measured in loss of quality of life and higher risks of health hazards. We could put a number in dollars on these costs, but it would not do it justice. We would and will live in a very different world from the one today. Some of nature's wonders will be gone forever, the cost of which is impossible to calculate. It is in our hands to stop climate change and transform our economy so that it is sustainable.

A meaningful endowment of resources at birth ensures that children can realize their potential. We all have different things that we value, and we need resources to develop our personal capabilities.[13] It is not enough to have some abstract "freedom". Those who love sports need sports equipment, those who love music need musical instruments, those who love engineering need tools, and so on. Again, what matters here are resources. The government should ensure that those children that do not have enough resources can get them. This should not be beyond what a government could do.

Secure retirement is important to reduce anxiety in the society. Many Americans are living on low incomes and hence are not able to save much. The bottom 50% have 3.44 trillion dollars in wealth, compared to 18 trillion dollars owned by the top 0.1% and 40 trillion dollars by the 50–90 percentile

---

[12] https://www.cdc.gov/nchs/pressroom/nchs_press_releases/2022/20220831.htm.
[13] https://plato.stanford.edu/entries/capability-approach/.

group.[14] This means that half of Americans face relative poverty in old age. The government could deliver public pensions that lift millions of old-age Americans out of poverty. Can we afford it? It depends on whether the US economy can produce the goods and services that the pensioners would buy with their increased incomes.

Sound banking and financial services, an equitable and economically fair justice system, and recreation and participation in civic and democratic life are not a question of whether we can afford them in terms of resources. The question that we face is whether we have the political will to build the institutions that can deliver these results. This will take time and long periods of trial and error, during which voters will get their say on what policies they like and which they don't like.

---

[14] https://www.federalreserve.gov/releases/z1/dataviz/dfa/distribute/table/.

7

Outlook

Not least because of the corona pandemic and its economic effects, we have come to realize that the federal government spends *our* money. In doing so, it uses our resources for the public purpose. This includes the provision of public goods in areas such as education and infrastructure, spending to combat climate change and fight poverty, and much more. The old tales of taxpayers' money and the supposed "financing" of government spending through taxes and sales of government bonds have had their day. We should replace existing political rules that supposedly limit government spending by setting a debt ceiling or using PAYGO rules with new rules, targeting a sustainable economy, full employment, and price stability.

The limit of the economy is not the availability of money. Money is "only" a legal construct to move resources. Money is not subject to "scarcity". Money is subject to political rules which control the access to resources. These rules can be adapted to the particular problems of society:

Whatever we can produce can be financed!

The limit of production lies in the availability of our resources. Firstly, these are limited, and secondly, their use generates side effects for our environment. We bear responsibility for this. In today's age of man-made climate change, the so-called Anthropocene, we have to decide which of our resources we want to use to what extent and for what purpose. The economy should adapt to the environment, not the other way around.

Full employment, price stability, and the Green New Deal

With its economic policy instruments—including monetary and fiscal policy—the state has effective levers at its disposal to achieve its goals. Full employment can be achieved when the federal government adjusts its spending accordingly and, in the future, introduces a Job Guarantee. In this way, overall economic spending will permanently reach a level that adjusts the number of jobs to the number of job seekers. An economic bill of rights can give guidance to the federal government what the people expect from it. The private sector keeps doing what it's doing, delivering goods and services of high quality and fair prices. It is the federal government's task to ensure that the private sector delivers. If it does not, regulation should be updated to ensure that profits can only be made when private firm create value for citizens.

The most important project in the coming decades is a Green New Deal, i.e., a socio-ecological transformation. Here, the government and the private sector should work together to drive forward the transformation toward an environmentally sustainable economy. Gross domestic product (GDP) growth will take a back seat. In the first half of 2020, we have seen all over the world that life is worth living even without non-essential consumption. We don't need Caribbean cruises or weekend trips to Las Vegas to lead a free, meaningful, and self-determined life. There is no right to destroy the livelihood of some communities with one's own consumption. However, less consumption would currently result in higher unemployment, which is socially unacceptable. The state can eliminate this unemployment through additional spending and cuts in working hours. Given that an update to crucial infrastructure is needed and that demographic changes will mean that there will be less workers available, running out of work does not seem to be a threat.

Any resulting public deficits are just the flipside of households and firms having a surplus of income over expenditure, allowing them to financially net save. It means that we have more money and can therefore pay more taxes in the future. Modern money is nothing else than a tax credit that we can use to pay our taxes. Reducing the federal debt is neither necessary nor useful. A person or a company can pay off debt by transferring money to creditors. The state cannot. When it transfers money to the creditors, i.e., the private sector, its expenditures and thus its debt increase! Conversely, when its creditors or its citizens increase their spending on taxes, its debts decrease. The state can only reduce its debt when it receives more tax revenues!

Price stability can be achieved by the federal government adjusting its spending to the economic situation so that wage growth minus productivity growth approaches the inflation target. If energy prices cause a rise in the rate of inflation, the government should ensure a steady supply of energy at constant prices. It can try to replace foreign energy imports with sustainable energy generated at home. In the case of energy prices going up the government is not able to bring down resulting inflation directly. A rise in the interest rate will certainly not help to sort out the problem of high energy prices. It might even reduce private investment in that sector, leading to less supply and even higher energy prices in the future, while adding to demand through higher interest payments on the public debt.

If aggregate demand in the economy is too high and causing inflation (bottlenecks will arise before full employment is reached), the government should deal with the scarcity problem that this indicates. If workers are scarce, it could postpone some of its non-urgent investment projects to free workers for other employment (if that helps with reducing wage pressures). Public investments can be pulled forward if demand in the economy as a whole is weak and construction workers idle. Alternatively, private investment can be increased through changes in regulation. This can be done by changing banking regulation as well as by prohibiting speculative investment in areas that are not clearly a benefit for the citizens.

Working time and distribution

If, with existing working hours, consumption triggers an unacceptably high level of resource consumption, the working week can be shortened. It was around 60 h at the beginning of the twentieth century and has fallen to slightly below 40 h since the end of the last century. It would therefore be easy to imagine using the higher productivity of our workforces to reduce the working week, among other things. A four-day week would certainly be a good first step in this direction.

Finally, we should also rethink the distribution of income and wealth (see Fig. 7.1). All citizens should earn income on a regular basis. This would go a long way to eradicate poverty. Disproportionately high income and wealth generate political power that is incompatible with a democratic system. Proposals for an inheritance tax and a wealth tax should help us to redress the distribution of income and wealth. The result should be a society in which economic development pushes all boats upward. No communities should be excluded from social development. Banks and financial markets must be regulated to prevent undeservedly high incomes and wealth.

Shaping the future

Understanding the modern monetary system has political implications. As a democratically constituted society, we are much more powerful than we thought. We do not have to passively accept globalization, the dismantling of

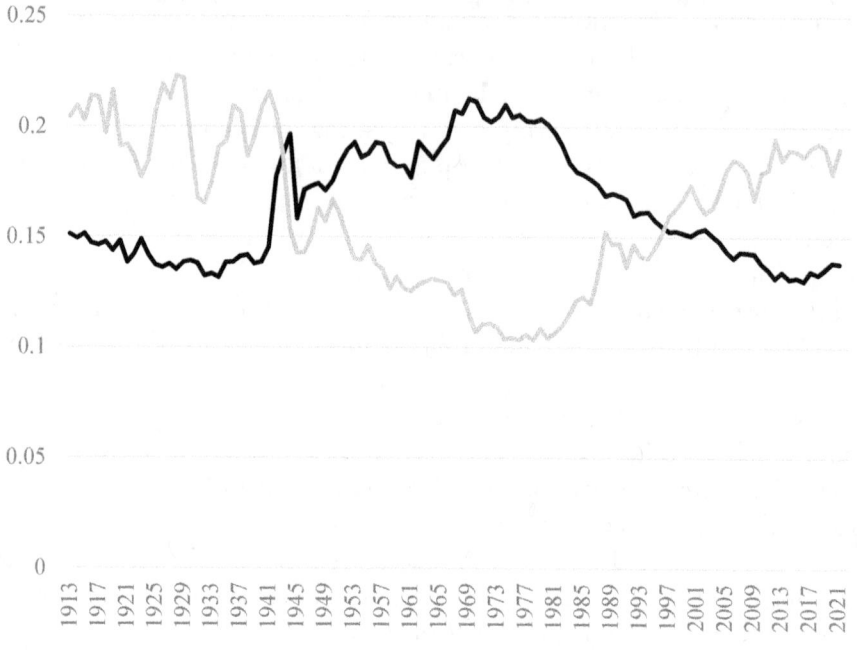

Fig. 7.1 Pre-tax national income of bottom 50% (black) and top 1% (gray) of adults as a share in total income. *Source* World Inequality Database

unions, the liberalization of (financial) markets, the reduction of wages, and the scaling back of the welfare state. Through democracy, we can shape our society according to our values, including the goals of full employment, price stability, and a sustainable economy.

We do not need to rely on the rich or taxpayers to achieve our goals. We do not need taxes to increase government spending. Nor do we need financial markets and banks to finance our government. We can simply change the rules, as we have done during the pandemic. National governments simply spend as much as they feel is politically justified. This spending will be written into the budget, which will be approved by Congress. Politicians will not want to create inflation because it is politically unpopular. This is why they will not draw more resources from the private sector to the public sector than absolutely necessary.

We decide how much of our money is spent. We decide how to use our resources. Of course, our generation will make new mistakes in the process, which in turn will require new solutions. We must be radical, however, to secure that change can and should happen—and not be satisfied with "business as usual". We must forge new paths to preserve our communities and address the great challenges of our time. The good news is that whatever we want to do, we'll always be able to "pay for it".

Literature

Attewell, Steven. 2018. *People Must Live by Work: Direct Job Creation in America, from FDR to Reagan.* Philadelphia: University of Pennsylvania Press

Binder, Sarah and Mark Spindel. 2017. *The Myth of Independence: How Congress Governs the Federal Reserve.* Princeton: Princeton University Press

Clarida, Richard H., Burcu Duygan-Bump, and Chiara Scotti (2021), „The COVID-19 Crisis and the Federal Reserve's Policy Response," Finance and Economics Discussion Series 2021-035. Washington: Board of Governors of the Federal Reserve System, https://doi.org/10.17016/FEDS.2021.035

Desan, Christine. 2014. *Making Money: Coin, Currency, and the Coming of Capitalism.* Oxford: Oxford University Press

Earle, Joe, Cahal Moran and Zach Ward-Perkins. 2017. The Econocracy: The perils of leaving economics to the experts. Manchester: Manchester University Press

Ehnts, Dirk. 2008. *Foreign Direct Investment, Linkages and Spillovers in a New Economic Geography Framework.* Hamburg: Bod Verlag

Ehnts, Dirk. 2017. *Modern Monetary Theory and European Macroeconomics.* Basingstoke: Routledge

Ehnts, Dirk. 2022. *Modern Money Theory: Eine Einführung.* Wiesbaden: Springer

Ehnts, Dirk. 2023. *Makroökonomik: Wirtschaftstheorie für das 21. Jahrhundert.* Wiesbaden: Springer

Ehnts, Dirk. 2019. The balance sheet approach to macroeconomics, in: Samuel Decker, Wolfram Elsner, Svenja Flechtner (eds.), *Principles and Pluralist Approaches in Teaching Economics – Towards a Transformative Science*, Basingstoke: Routledge

Ehnts, Dirk and Erik Jochem (2020), Why Pufendorf Matters, in: Jürgen G. Backhaus, Günther Chaloupek, Hans A. Frambach (Hrsg.), *Samuel Pufendorf and the Emergence of Economics as a Social Science*, Basel: Springer

Ehnts, Dirk and Maurice Höfgen. 2019. The Job Guarantee: Full Empoyment, Price Stability and Social Progress. *Society Register* 3(2), 49–65

Ehnts, Dirk and Michael Paetz. 2021. COVID-19 and its economic consequences for the Euro Area, *Eurasian Economic Review* 11, 227–249

Eich, Stefan. 2022. *The Currency of Politics: The Political Theory of Money from Aristotle to Keynes.* Princeton: Princeton University Press

Feinig, Jakob. 2022. *Moral Economies of Money: Politics and the Monetary Constitution of Society.* Stanford: Stanford University Press

Forstater, Mathew and Warren Mosler. 2005. The Natural Rate of Interest is Zero. *Journal of Economic Issues* 34 (2), pp. 535–542

Forstater, Mathew and Michael J. Murray. 2013. *The Job Guarantee – toward true Full Employment.* New York: Palgrave Macmillan

Fullwiler, Scott. 2017. Modern central bank operations: the general principles, in: Louis-Philippe Rochon and Sergio Rossi (eds.), *Advances in Endogenous Money Analysis,* 50–87, Cheltenham: Edward Elgar

Grey, Rohan. 2020. Administering Money: Coinage, Debt Crises, and the Future of Fiscal Policy, *Kentucky Law Journal* 109(29), 229–298

Grubb, Farley. 2018. Colonial Virginia's paper money, 1755–1774: value decomposition and performance, *Financial History Review* 25(2), 113–140

Heine, Michael und Hansjörg Herr. 2021. *The European Central Bank.* London: Agenda Publishing

Höfgen, Maurice. 2020. Mythos Geldknappheit: Modern Monetary Theory oder Warum es am Geld nicht scheitern muss, Stuttgart: Schäffer-Poeschel

IWF. 2019. IMF Country report 19/124. Germany: Selected Issues. https://www.elibrary.imf.org/view/IMF002/21505-9781498328524/21505-9781498328524/21505-9781498328524_A001.xml

Kaboub, Fadhel. 2007. ELR-led Economic Development: A Plan for Tunesia. Levy Economics Institute working paper 499

Keen, Steve. 2021. The appallingly bad neoclassical economics of climate change, *Globalizations* 18(7), pp. 1149–1177. https://doi.org/10.1080/14747731.2020.1807856

Kelton, Stephanie. 2020. *The Deficit Myth: Modern Monetary Theory and the Birth of the People's Economy.* New York: Public Affairs

Keynes, John Maynard. 1963 [1935]. A Self-Adjusting Economic System. *Nebraska Journal of Economics and Business* 2(2), 11–15

Keynes, John Maynard. 1936. *A General Theory of Employment, Interest and Money.* London: Macmillan

Knapp, Georg Friedrich (1924) [1905] *The State Theory of Money*, abridged and translated by H. M. Lucas and J. Bonar. London: Macmillan

Lerner, Abba. 1943. Functional Finance and the Federal Debt, *Social Research* 10 (1), pp. 38–51

Marx, Karl. 1914 [1867] *Das Kapital: Kritik der politischen Ökonomie*, book 1, Stuttgart: Dietz

Mazzucato, Mariana. 2021. *Mission Economy: A Moonshot Guide to Changing Capitalism.* New York: Harper

Minsky, Hyman. 2008. *Stabilizing and Unstable Economy*, New York: McGraw-Hill Education

Mitchell, William und Joan Muysken. 2008. *Full Employment Abandoned: Shifting Sands and Policy Failures.* Cheltenham: Edward Elgar

Mitchell, William. 2017a. *Eurozone Dystopia: Groupthink and Denial on a Grand Scale* Cheltenham: Edward Elgar

Mitchell, William und Thomas Fazi. 2017b. *Reclaiming the State: A Progressive Vision of Sovereignty for a Post-Neoliberal World*, London: Pluto Press

Mitchell, William, Randall Wray und Martin Watts. 2019. *Macroeconomics.* London: Red Globe

Mosler, Warren. 1995. Soft currency economics. https://econpapers.repec.org/paper/wpawuwpma/9502007.htm

Mosler, Warren. 1998. Full Employment and Price Stability. *Journal of post-Keynesian Economics* 20(2), pp. 167–182

Mosler, Warren. 2010. *The 7 Deadly Innocent Frauds of Economic Policy.* Christiansted, VI: Valance Co Inc

Nersisyan, Yeva und L. Randall Wray. 2021. Has Japan Been Following Modern Monetary Theory Without Recognizing It? Levy Economics Institute working paper 985

Raworth, Kate. 2017. *Doughnut Economics: 7 Ways to Trhink Like a 21st Century Economist.* London: Chelsea Green Pub

Schumpeter, Joseph. 2021 [1912]. *Theory of Economic Development.* London: Routledge

Smith, Adam. 1776. *An Inquiry into the Nature and Causes of the Wealth of Nations.* London: W. Strahan and T. Cadell

Tcherneva, Pavlina. 2020. *The Case for a Job Guarantee.* New York: Polity

Thatcher, Margaret. 1983. Speech to Conservative Party Conference. https://www.margaretthatcher.org/document/105454

Turner, Adair. 2015. *Between Debt and the Devil: Money, Credit, and Fixing Global Finance.* Princeton: Princeton University Press

Watts, Martin. 2021. The methodology for assessing interest-rate policy rules: some comments. *European Journal of Economics and Economic Policies: Intervention* 18(3), pp. 275–285

Weber, Isabella. 2021. *How China Escaped Shock Therapy: The Market Reform Debate.* Basingstoke: Routledge

Weber, Isabella and Wasner, Evan. 2023. Sellers' Inflation, Profits and Conflict: Why can Large Firms Hike Prices in an Emergency?, UMass Amherst Economics Department Working Paper Series 343

Wray, Randall. 2012. Global Financial Crisis: A Minskyan Interpretation of the Causes, the Fed's Bailout, and the Future. Levy Economics Institute working paper 711

Wray, Randall. 2014. *Modern Money Theory: A Primer on Macroeconomics for Sovereign Monetary Systems*. Basingstoke: Palgrave Macmillan

Wray, Randall. 2022. *Making Money Work for Us: How MMT Can Save America*, New York: Polity Books

GPSR Compliance

The European Union's (EU) General Product Safety Regulation (GPSR) is a set of rules that requires consumer products to be safe and our obligations to ensure this.

If you have any concerns about our products, you can contact us on

ProductSafety@springernature.com

In case Publisher is established outside the EU, the EU authorized representative is:

Springer Nature Customer Service Center GmbH
Europaplatz 3
69115 Heidelberg, Germany

www.ingramcontent.com/pod-product-compliance
Lightning Source LLC
LaVergne TN
LVHW011008250326
834688LV00004B/136